# The Externally Focused Quest

# The Externally Focused Quest

## Becoming the Best Church for the Community

Eric Swanson and Rick Rusaw

Foreword by Alan Hirsch

FORTRESS PRESS
MINNEAPOLIS

THE EXTERNALLY FOCUSED QUEST
Becoming the Best Church for the Community

Copyright © 2020 Fortress Press edition, an imprint of 1517 Media. Minor text revisions are new for the 2020 Fortress Press edition.

First edition copyright © 2007 by John Wiley & Sons, Inc. All rights reserved.

Cover Image: iStock © 2019; Help, Community, People in a Row Holding Hands with the typescript stock illustration by KeithBishop
Cover Design: Alisha Lofgren

Print ISBN: 978-1-5064-6345-2
Ebook ISBN: 978-1-5064-6346-9

*To the next generation: Gentry, Jenda, Blaise, Lincoln, Titus, Violet, Maelie, and Saylor May. Now it's your turn to figure it out.*

—E. S.

*To the LifeBridge family. Thanks for your friendship and encouragement. You have risked, loved, and seen beyond the walls of our church and are making a difference in our community. It has been a privilege to journey with you.*

—R. R.

# Contents

# Contents

# Foreword

One of the axioms of leadership that we can assume is that *every organization is perfectly designed to achieve what it is currently achieving.* This comment usually raises a bit of pushback because it seems to put responsibility for any current situation back onto those who lead the organization. And this is in some ways true, but it's only half the truth. It also suggests that there is something in the inherited ecclesial templates handed down, and subsequently adopted without serious critical reflection, that tends to factor in the propensity for either growth or decline. So, the issues do concentrate around leadership imagination and inherent design flaws in the way we conceive of, and do, church.

If your church is in decline, it is probably because you are organizationally designed for it. Don't complain . . . redesign! And you need to redesign along the lines that Jesus intended. You see, the church that Jesus built is *designed* for growth—and massive, highly transformative growth at that. It was Jesus who said, "I will build my church, and the gates of Hades will not prevail against it" (Matt 16:18). Hang on! It says that the gates of hell don't prevail against us! It is the church that is on the advance here, not hell! Contrary to many of the images of church as some sort of a defensive fortress under the terrible, relentless onslaughts of hell, the church that Jesus built is designed to be an advancing, untamed and untamable, revolutionary force created to transform the world. And make no mistake: there is in Jesus's words here a real sense of inevitability about the eventual triumph of the gospel. If we are not somehow part of this, then there is something wrong in the prevailing designs and they must change.

The reality is that the Western church is in a precarious situation today. Missional observation in Australia indicates that between 12 and 15 percent of the population will likely be attracted to the prevailing contemporary church-growth model. This is not actual attendance, which is way below this figure (around 2.8 percent); rather, it indicates "market appeal" or cultural connectivity. The rest of the population, most of whom describe themselves as "spiritually open," will probably never find their place in a contemporary attractional church. It is simply out of their cultural orbit. If they are not repulsed by it, they are at least blasé and/or turned off to the cultural forms inherent in the model.

In the United States the situation is not much better. I estimate that in the United States the percentage of people who find their spiritual connection through an attractional church is probably up to 40 percent. Again, this is not attendance, which is more around 18 percent.

In both countries, the demographics of the group likely to "come to church" are probably what we can call the inspirational middle-class, family-values segment—good, solid, well-educated, hard-working, suburbanites with Republican leanings. Contemporary attractional churches are really effective in reaching non-

Christian people fitting this demographic, but it is unlikely that they can reach far beyond that—leaving about 60 percent of the population out of the equation. So, the question we must ask is, "How will the 60 percent of our population access the gospel if they reject the current expression of church?"

This is precisely the issue that the missional church seeks to address. My contention is that it is going to take an "externally focused" approach to church that is both missional and incarnational in order to reach beyond the 40 percenters. It is only when the church decides to become the best church *for* the community that it at least has a fighting chance to reach the majority of the unchurched/dechurched population. The attractional church is about getting the community into the church. The missional, externally focused church is about getting the church into the community. Incarnational ministry, at its heart, is taking church to people by helping believers live out their calling among people who do not yet believe and follow Jesus.

The missional, externally focused church begins with missionary questions: "What is good news for this people group?"; "What would the church look and feel like among this people group?" Entering into a community through love, service, and blessing creates new proximate spaces as we become good news to the community. At the end of the day the impact of a church is not determined by who it wants to reach but by who it is willing to serve. Certainly, missional living affects what happens outside the church, but it also greatly affects our own spiritual formation as disciples of Jesus. *The Externally Focused Quest* provides a significant part of the answer to the question of how we turn religious consumers into missional disciples who can impact the world around them for Jesus's cause.

Building on the already significant insights from their previous writings, Eric and Rick blend years of direct leadership experience with great theological insights and a real heart for missional impact, and so concoct a really good book for our time. Our appropriate compliment ought to be to follow their advice, move into our communities, and transform them in Jesus's name.

—Alan Hirsch
Los Angeles, January 2020
Missional author, dreamer, and strategist
www.theforgottenways.org

# Preface

*As difficult as it is to learn to surf, it is far easier to catch a wave than to cause a wave.*

Everywhere we go, we meet people who, after listening to either of us speak on externally focused church, will say something like, "What you said today was exactly what I've been thinking, but I didn't have the terminology or diagrams to explain it." There is a movement of God taking place, and as we often say, "As difficult as it is to learn to surf, it is far easier to catch a wave than to cause a wave." When God is causing such a wave, we can stand on the pier and let it break over us, or we can grab a surfboard, hit the surf, and have the ride of our lives. What will you do?

When we wrote *The Externally Focused Church* in 2004 and the first edition of this book in 2009, we invited our readers to think differently about what church could and should be. We included nearly every church we were aware of that was loving and ministering outside its walls. Over the years, the externally focused church movement has matured to the extent that projects and initiatives that were rare in 2004 are now quite common in 2020. Believers are longing to do something besides take notes in a worship service. Thousands of churches are rediscovering the DNA of the gospel and are living the gospel outside the walls of the church. Since we started this journey, we have been with scores of churches and thousands of people around the world, have listened to their stories, and have tried to allow their experiences to deepen our own thinking about God's missional and incarnational design in the world. What we have discovered is contained in the nine missional paradigms that we write about here, and we believe they can determine what impact you will have on our changing world. For those of you who are new to the journey, we say, "Grab your board and get ready for the ride of your life!"

Christian magazines love publishing lists of the best churches—"The 100 Largest Churches," "The 50 Most Innovative Churches," "The 50 Fastest-Growing Churches," and so on. Some pastors whose churches make these coveted lists often frame and hang these outcomes to display to the world that they are doing a good job. But what if "largest," "most innovative," and "fastest-growing" were the wrong measures? Is there something else we could be working toward?

One good question changes things. One great question has the power to change a life, a church, a community, and potentially the world. When we wrote *The Externally Focused Church*, our big provocative question was "If your church were to close its doors, would anyone in the community notice—would anyone in the community care?" It is no coincidence that this question set many church leaders on a journey, a quest. It is no coincidence that the word *question* comes from the same root as *quest*—a journey in search of something important. So, let's think of questions as the beginning of a quest of discovery. Jesus was a master at asking great questions. "What will a man give in exchange for his soul?" "Who do you say I am?" "What good is salt if it has lost its flavor?" "Do you believe I am able to do this?" "Do you want to be well?" "Why are you so fearful?" How we answer such questions shapes our lives and our futures.

We've discovered that questions are malleable and that rearranging a word here or there can result in a totally different answer.

"Pastor, may I smoke while I'm praying?"

"No!"

"Pastor, while I'm smoking, is it OK if I pray?"

"Why, that would be a wonderful idea!"

Changing the beneficiary of a question is a powerful way to transform a question to a quest. As Martin Luther King Jr. noted, the question that the good Samaritan asked was not "If I stop to help this man, what will happen to me?" but "If I *do not* stop to help this man, what will happen to *him*?"[1] A powerful question has implications for life. John F. Kennedy adapted a phrase in such a way that, a half-century later, the question we should be asking still resonates: "Ask not what your country can do for you—ask what you can do for your country."[2]

Most churches, blatantly or subtly, have an unspoken objective—"How can we be the 'best church *in* our community'?"—and they staff, budget, and plan accordingly. How a church answers that question determines its entire approach to its members, staff, prayers, finances, time, technology, and facilities. But becoming an externally focused church is not about becoming the best church *in* the community. The externally focused church asks, "How can we be the best church *for* our community?" That one little preposition changes everything. And this is the big question this book seeks to answer. This is your question; this is your quest.

We have written the book around nine big missional concepts that need to be addressed in your quest to become the best church for the community—focus, purpose, story, missions, partnering, systems, evangelism, creativity, and outcomes. Understanding and applying the truths of each concept will provide many of the tools you will need for your externally focused quest. We can't guarantee that it will be easy to attain, but then again, things that we value and cherish rarely are. We're glad you've picked up this book. We're glad you've joined the journey. It's going to be a great ride.

# 1.

# What Kind of Day Is Today?

*The church must forever be asking, "What kind of day is it today?" for no two days are alike in her history.*

—David Smith, *Mission after Christendom*[1]

A few years ago, I (Eric) met a young pastor named Jeff Waldo from University Baptist Church, outside of Houston. Jeff had just finished a master's program in Future Studies from the University of Houston. After the disappointing discovery that he knew nothing of horoscopes, crystal balls, tarot cards, or fortune cookies, Jeff told me what future studies was about. Future Studies is not about prediction but about imagining plausible and possible scenarios for the future so that we can plan accordingly. "If things continue along this trajectory, this is what we can expect." Of course, the future rarely has the decency to conform to our expectations, and prognosticators are notoriously bad at predicting future outcomes. As Yogi Berra used to say, "It's difficult to make predictions . . . especially about the future." Consider this prediction regarding television. In 1946 film mogul Darryl F. Zanuck of 20th Century Fox said, "Television won't be able to hold on to any market it captures after the first six months. People will soon get tired of staring at a plywood box every night."[2] In 2007 Steve Ballmer, CEO of Microsoft predicted, "There's no chance that the iPhone is going to get any significant market share. No chance."[3]

Just how accurately can anyone predict the future? If anyone should know, it would be Phillip Tetlock. For twenty years, this psychology professor at the University of California, Berkeley, worked with 284 people who made their living as "experts" in prognostication about politics and economics. By the end of the study, the experts had made 82,361 forecasts, placing most of the forecasting questions into three possible future outcomes: things would stay the same (status quo), get better (political freedom, economic growth), or get worse (repression, recession). What was the outcome? Statistically untrained chimps, with a dartboard, would have come up with more accurate predictions![4]

Predicting the future is not our goal here, but discovering today's trends and patterns is. Why? Those discoveries do help shape tomorrow and enlighten us. We must wake up and ask ourselves, "What kind of day is today?"

1

## STEEPR: A Leadership Skill to Master

To understand the times and to be in step with what God is doing, all leaders need the ability to answer the question "What kind of day is today?" You probably remember the men of Issachar from 1 Chronicles 12:32 "who understood the times and [therefore] knew what Israel should do." In Luke 12:54–56, Jesus poses this question to the crowd: "When you see a cloud rising in the west, immediately you say, 'It's going to rain,' and it does. And when the south wind blows, you say, 'It's going to be hot,' and it is. Hypocrites! You know how to interpret the appearance of the earth and the sky. How is it that you *don't know how to interpret this present time*?"

So how do futurists think about the future? Jeff identified the constructs he and other futurists use. The broad bellwether categories futurists pay attention to are society, technology, economics, environment, and politics. To these five categories Jeff insightfully adds religion—now forming the acronym STEEPR. Using these six categories helps us think about what kind of day it is. It helps us become men and women who interpret the present and know what new questions to ask and what changes to make. Let's take a brief snapshot, from a 30,000-foot altitude, of what kind of day it is today using the STEEPR approach.

### Society

In the past few years there have been at least three big societal shifts that affect how we interact with one another.

1. *The centers of trust are eroding and shifting.* Trust is the foundation of all human interactions. In 2018 Rachel Botsman released a best-selling book entitled *Who Can You Trust?* She puts forth the idea that over the centuries we have moved from relational trust, where everyone in a village personally knew who they could or could not trust, to institutional trust. The institutions of government, business, media, and even religion were once seen as bulwarks of trust. But as those institutions displayed their cracks, flaws, and sometimes criminal shortcomings, trust has become distributed. Rating systems now form the core of this trust revolution. So, a four-star recommendation by a thousand people on Yelp is more trusted than a local expert restaurant reviewer. Today ratings by our peers allow us to cross the trust threshold and rent a room from a stranger in the Czech Republic through Airbnb or take a ride to the airport in Mexico City through Uber, or purchase that set of headphones on Amazon or a picture frame from Craigslist.

In the past, clergy would be rated as one of the most trusted professions. Today the latest (2019) polls show that trust of clergy has dropped to an all-time low—below funeral directors but still above telemarketers and used car salesmen.[5] A 2018 Barna research project revealed that only 6 percent of Americans strongly trust that our government has their best interest at heart. Only 36 percent strongly trust that church has their best interest at heart.[6]

2. *Who is included in the American dream has changed.* When the framers of the Declaration of Independence penned the words "that all men are created equal, that they are endowed by their Creator with certain unalienable Rights, that among these are Life, Liberty and the pursuit of Happiness," they were referring primarily to white, male landowners. Over the decades the definition of "all men" has expanded to include Native Americans, African Americans, women, and most recently those of the LGBTQ community. Inclusion also is tied to tolerance and human rights that go beyond our borders.

Interestingly, the expansion of the early church was on a trajectory of inclusion. The church was birthed with new believers of thirteen language groups. Phillip expanded the church to include Samaritans and Ethiopians (Acts 8). Peter led a Roman Centurion and his family to Christ in Acts 10 and now they were part of the expanding, inclusive church. This concept of who could be included was so radical at the time that the early church leaders had to come together in Jerusalem to figure things out (Acts 15).

So how is the church to respond today? Who gets to be included in the kingdom dream? Black Lives Matter. The #MeToo and #ChurchToo movements beckon us to expand our circle of empathy and love. As personal, denominational, and regional battle lines are being drawn, it may be helpful to heed the wisdom of Bob Goff. In his book *Love Does*, he ponders what counsel Jesus would give. He writes, "[Jesus] said people who followed Him should think of themselves more like ushers rather than the bouncers, and it would be God who decides who gets in. We're the ones who simply show people to their seats that someone else paid for."[7] Are you an usher or a bouncer in the kingdom? Who is there a seat for in your kingdom dream? Who is excluded?

3. *Anxiety has risen.* The worldwide pandemic of the coronavirus (COVID-19) brought to light how fragile and vulnerable we are as a people. With a national state of emergency in force, countries were in lockdown, international travel was prohibited, schools were closed, and workers were encouraged to work from home. Disneyland closed, St. Patrick's Day parades and March Madness were cancelled. With professional and amateur sporting events and seasons cancelled, the global economy collapsing and churches, stadiums, theatres, restaurants, and arenas being closed, it's not difficult to understand why people would feel a corporate angst. Even before this tragic outbreak, however, Americans were growing more and more anxious. The American Psychiatric Association (APA) ran a poll of one thousand US residents in 2017 and found that nearly two-thirds were "extremely or somewhat anxious about health and safety for themselves and their families and more than a third are more anxious overall than last year."[8] In 2018 the APA ran another poll and discovered that anxiety had increased by another 5 percent. And apparently we Christ-followers are not exempt. Look at the most popular and shared scripture verses of the past three years. According to the YouVersion Bible app, in 2019 Philippians 4:6 was the most shared, highlighted, and bookmarked verse of the year: "Don't worry about anything; instead, pray about everything."

The most popular verse in 2018 was Isaiah 41:10, "Do not fear, for I am with you," and 2017's top verse was Joshua 1:9, "Do not be afraid; do not be discouraged."[9]

So, what is happening here? Although the causes are not definitive, here are a few possible candidates:

- We experience real external threats of domestic terrorism (think Boston Marathon bomber), mass shootings (think Sandy Hook, Orlando, or Las Vegas) and most recently the spread of deadly disease.

- A college degree no longer guarantees a great job. In recent times a college degree was the necessary ticket to punch on the way to the American dream. That is not the case today. Anxiety is highest among millennials,[10] and students who graduated from college in 2017 did so with an average debt of $28,650.[11]

- For cable news companies like CNN and Fox to create loyal viewership, every episode needs enough drama for viewers to stay tuned for the next host or the next day to discover what is unfolding in the twenty-four-hour news cycle. We are led to believe that selecting the wrong president or Supreme Court justice would be the beginning of the apocalypse. Never-ending drama can often lead to never-ending stress and anxiety about the future.

- The use of social media has risen. Especially among younger people, social media use leads to comparison, cyber-bullying, FOMO (fear of missing out), less sleep, depression, and in some cases suicide. A study of over 400,000 adults revealed that between 2008 and 2017 there was a "71 percent increase in young adults experiencing serious psychological distress in the previous 30 days."[12] A 2019 Barna study shows that the people who say they are lonely or isolated has doubled in the past decade . . . from 10 percent to 20 percent.[13] Just one in three eighteen- to thirty-five-year-old respondents tells Barna they often feel deeply cared for by those around them (33 percent) or that someone believes in them (32 percent).[14]

What's changing in your social world that presents new opportunities for God to show up in fresh ways?

## Technology

The four horsemen that are driving the tech revolution are bandwidth (how much data can be sent over a specific connection in a specific time), speed (the rate at which data is computed and transferred), storage (how much information can be stored and where it is stored), and data (specifically how data is gathered and the role of machine learning to make sense of it). There are at least five ways technology shapes our lifestyle today.

First is *how we access information*. Gone are the days when we had to argue about a sports statistic or record and had no way of checking who was correct. Gone are the days when we had persistent curiosity about something we wondered about. Virtually anything we want to know about is available within seconds. Google's corporate mission is "to organize the world's information and make it universally accessible and useful."[15] Their vision is "to provide access to the world's information in one click."[16] If you want to know how to do something, like change the time on your car's dashboard, frost a cake, dance, or place an ad on Facebook, most likely you will find very helpful instructional videos on YouTube created by passionate devotees.

News stories, once the purview of reporters and telejournalists, are increasingly broken by common folk with a cell phone. In May 2008, the earthquake that devastated Sichuan, China, was reported as it happened via cell phones and social media sites. The BBC reportedly heard of the quake via Twitter. The communication was powerful and instant. By contrast, in previous times, the government would have taken months to even disclose that an earthquake had occurred. In the summer of 2009, hundreds of Iranians used cell phone video cameras to capture the dissent of thousands of Iranians expressing their reaction to a flawed election. Today Twitter seems to be the medium to first report things like the Boston Marathon bombing in 2015, or the Hudson River plane crash that same year. Today political candidates announce their candidacy on Twitter and elected officials make their opinions known through this same medium. If you find yourself saying, "This is old news!"—and by the time you read this, it will be—you only help drive home the point of how quickly our world is changing.

Accessing information also affects *how we are educated*. In 2019 over 230,000 students were working on their college degrees by taking all their classes online through the University of Phoenix. Nearly two hundred US universities, including Harvard, Yale, Stanford, MIT, and Cal Berkeley offer free online courses through various learning platforms like Udemy, edX, and Coursera. Twenty-three percent of all adults and 42 percent of millennials listen to at least one podcast each month.[17]

Second is *how information accesses us*. Everything we buy, everything we search for on our screens, everything we post, every place we go, every "Like" we click, every emoji we post leaves a trail of digital exhaust that reveals our interests, motivations, personality type, buyer intent, etc. Our "behavioral surplus" forms the raw material that leads to personalized offerings. Twenty years ago, we searched Google. Today it is Google that searches us. In 2012 *Forbes* posted an article titled "How Target Figured Out a Teen Girl Was Pregnant before Her Father Did."[18] The article was a primer on how machine learning and predictive analytics work. Target has a baby registry on which expectant moms can register and post their due date. Target then tracks what these moms-to-be purchase each trimester of their pregnancy. Other pregnant women who shop at Target but do not register in the baby registry buy the same products in the same time frameworks as the future moms who have registered. Having access to this data, Target is able to predict with 87 percent accuracy not only that a woman is pregnant but also her due date within two weeks. Data and messaging like this explain why each of us receives differing ads/offers in the mail or sees different marketing messages on our Facebook feed than our friends see, or why different products are even placed in our favorite TV shows.[19]

Most of us actually like the fact that Amazon and Netflix create suggestions of what we might want to consume based on our past purchases or viewing. The better they *know* us, the better they can *match* us to what we are looking for.

Third, technology affects *how we connect and communicate* with one another. The smartphone changed everything. Today nearly every adult in America and much of the world carriers a smartphone that serves as a phone, email server, web browser, messaging service, camera, video recorder, and navigation system. Add to these basic features over 4.8 million apps that can be downloaded on Apple or Android smartphones.[20] If you can imagine it, there's probably an app for it. This amazing handheld piece of technology allows us to connect and communicate as never before. In 2019 we sent over 293 billion emails to one another each and every day.[21] That's over thirty-eight emails per day for every man, woman, and child on the planet. Worldwide, we sent 2.29 trillion text messages to one another in 2019.[22] We have access to personalized emojis and GIFs that serve as a new and effective form of shorthand.

A conversation on how we connect with one another would not be complete without mentioning how we communicate with machines. Alexa, Siri, and Google Assistant have become our handmaidens to take care of the everyday tasks of reading email, sending texts, creating shopping lists, setting alarms, doing math, checking facts, finding showtimes, starting the dishwasher, and thousands of other mundane things. The "God of all comfort" (2 Cor 1:3) takes on a new meaning with so many labor-saving functions at hand.

Some of you remember a time when you had to restrict your long-distance calling (anyone out of your area code) to evenings or Sundays before six p.m. because a long-distance call was crazy expensive. A typical call ended with, "Well, we better get off now since this is long-distance." Today we connect individually and visually around the world through FaceTime or at the office through Zoom for virtually zero cost. We keep in touch with a circle of friends through Facebook, Instagram, Twitter, and LinkedIn. Social media is more than huge, and it will continue to shape generations to come. Our friend Grant Skeldon observes, "Young believers spend more time on social media in one day than they spend in church in a month."[23] What opportunity does that present to kingdom-minded people?

Fourth, technology affects *how we entertain ourselves*. We used to go to the movies. Today the movies stream to us via Netflix, Amazon Prime, Disney Plus, Hulu, etc., and come to us via four types of screens—television, smartphones, computer screens, and tablets. Americans spend over 42 percent of their waking hours in front of one of those screens. Video technology allows us to watch consecutive episodes in one sitting. "In the summer of 2013, all the episodes [of] Season 4 of Arrested Development (TV series) [were] released on Netflix, and 10%

of their viewers watched the entire season in 24 hours."[24] Nearly 400,000 people watched all nine episodes of the second season of Netflix's hit *Stranger Things* within twenty-four hours of its release.[25] Binge-watching is here to stay.

Entertainment has to also include gaming, with average gamers spending over an hour per day playing online games.[26] Rather than making generational comparisons of how you spent your spare time back in the day ("What I could do with a yo-yo back in the day would blow your mind!"), it may be relevant to note that moderate amounts of gaming improve coordination, memory, attention, problem solving, and even social skills in children.[27]

Fifth, technology also affects the democratization of *who can create and contribute*. Web-based programs and phone-based apps mean that anyone has the ability to create the next big thing or spread their own ideas. The gatekeepers have left their posts because the gates have crumbled. At just thirteen years old, Justin Bieber was posting his music on YouTube when he was "discovered" by an agent who signed him with his new record label that he had formed with recording artist Usher. The rest, as they say, is history. Bieber has since sold over 150 million records.

Chancelor Bennett, aka Chance the Rapper, launched his music career by giving his music away for free. Since 2012 his music has been streamed over 1.5 billion times, and he has made his millions through live shows, merchandise, and endorsements instead of through music sales.[28] Anyone with a smartphone can create music, entertainment, or instructional videos and influence the world. As crazy as it sounds, in 2018 Business Insider ran an article titled "A Seven-Year Old Boy Is Making $22 Million a Year on YouTube Reviewing Toys."[29] The top ten YouTube stars made over $10 million each in 2018. If it's good, unique, or entertaining, the world will probably see it.

Going forward, technology will increasingly disrupt and shape how we live, work, learn, and play. Self-driving cars, facial-recognition systems, block-chain technology, virtual reality, and the ubiquity of connected devices (the Internet of Things) will increasingly become adopted and shape our everyday lives. Who knows?—maybe someday drones *will* actually deliver our packages from Amazon.

## Economics

Economic factors include how people make and spend money and the growth of national economies. In March 2020 the world shuttered as the ripple effects of the coronavirus (COVID-19) shredded the global economy. The world woke up to this Black Swan[30] event that resulted in empty grocery shelves and 401k retirement plans looking more like 201k plans. In spite of this economic setback, globally, there is little doubt that the United States is still the economic juggernaut of the world. As of 2019, with less than 5 percent of the world's population, the United States produced over 23 percent of global gross domestic product (GDP), followed by China producing over 15 percent of global GDP.[31] America has "more cars than licensed drivers" and "spends more on trash bags than ninety other countries spend on everything."[32]

To understand what is happening economically today, one has to consider what is happening with globalization. Globalization is the interconnectedness of people, goods, and services in the world. That your cell phone may have been designed in the United States and manufactured in China using components from Malaysia, Brazil, and Taiwan is symptomatic of globalization. And no job seems to be safe from export. Call the service department of almost any company, and it is very likely that you will be connected to Bangalore, India, or another of the call centers scattered around that country. Any job that can be outsourced either already has been or soon will be. Thomas Friedman, in a *New York Times* interview, noted, "When I was growing up, my parents used to say to me, 'Tom, finish your dinner. People in China and India are starving.' Today I tell my girls, 'Finish your homework. People in China and India are starving for your jobs.'"[33] We are now competing with workers on a global scale.

Consider some additional economic shifts.

### Rise of the gig economy

The gig economy is made up of full-time temporary contracted freelance workers as well as those full-time workers who also have a side-hustle job driving for Uber or doing part-time design work. Over a third of all workers in the US have some type of side-hustle gig.[34] If you are under forty, you probably have a side-hustle gig or are thinking about how you can get one.

### Growth of crowdsourcing

Crowdsourcing is based on a couple of well-known principles: 1) "No one of us is as smart as all of us";[35] and 2) "Given enough eyeballs, all bugs are shallow."[36] Companies like Procter & Gamble (P&G), which alone has thousands of researchers, are using crowdsourcing to solve their toughest problems. Rather than hiring more researchers, P&G is posting problems and challenges on the InnoCentive network, where 400,000 other scientists around the world (with over 60 percent holding advanced degrees) can help solve tough research-and-development (R&D) problems for cash rewards. Over 75 percent of the challenges are solved through crowdsourcing.[37]

### The rise of platform thinking

In 2015 Tom Goodwin, senior vice president of strategy and innovation at Havas Media, wrote a blog post that startled the business world:

> Uber, the world's largest taxi company, owns no vehicles. Facebook, the world's most popular media owner, creates no content. Alibaba, the most valuable retailer, has no inventory. And Airbnb, the world's largest accommodation provider, owns no real estate. Something interesting is happening.[38]

For the first time in history, value is separated from ownership. Powered by the internet, platforms are the best place to match in real time people who *want* something with people who *have* something. This match is called the "core interaction," and it is by multiplying the core interaction that platform enterprises grow and fulfill their mission. What is the one core interaction we want to grow and scale? Platform enterprises scale by turning consumers into producers as quickly as possible. So, you can ride with Uber today and drive for Uber tomorrow. Ideally, the only work platforms want to do is create tools that make the core interaction desirable, simple, repeatable, and common.

Platform thinking may even influence how we think about church.[39] Platform guru Sangeet Paul Choudary makes this observation:

> In an increasingly urbanized world, it is the creative class who is moving to the cities of the world, so most people sitting in churches in urban areas are part of the creative class—creating is part of their job all the time. When they come to church, they are consumers. They are sitting, listening to something, and constantly consuming. Some may have different levels of responsibility, but rules are regimented and curriculum driven, preventing creative production. Members of the creative class are not used to stepping into an environment where they are mere consumers of someone else's content. How could the church provide the tools and rules—non-regimented, non-strict—that enable every single participant to better leverage their creative abilities?

A church that equips members to live out their personal mission through business, the arts, education, public service, and other areas may reach and retain creatives.

How can you move from the consumer model to the contributor model? How can you help architect your church so that every person has the opportunity to contribute to the mission?

### How we buy stuff

How we buy stuff is changing. Who wants to get in the car and wrestle with traffic, only to find a limited selection of what you really want at the hardware store, sporting goods store, or department store? How much easier it is to open up Amazon and help fulfill founder Jeff Bezos's vision "to be Earth's most customer-centric company, where customers can find and discover anything they might want to buy online."[40] Amazon and other online retailers have shaped the way we buy. As a result, according to a Business Insider article posted November 8, 2019, retailers had announced more than 8,600 closings that year thus far, and a 2017 Credit Suisse report had predicted that between 20 percent and 25 percent of malls would close by 2022.[41]

Today we can order food at almost any restaurant and have it delivered via Grubhub or Uber Eats. Don't want to shop for groceries? For a nominal fee, most stores will do the shopping for you and have your groceries delivered to your front door.

*How we pay for things*

Cash is becoming a scarce item. Overall, about one-third, or 34 percent, of adults under the age of fifty make no purchases in a typical week using cash.[42] People of all ages, and especially younger generations, are increasingly moving toward payment methods like Apple Pay, Android Pay, Venmo, Zelle, or the Cash App. In China we may get a glimpse of America's future regarding how we pay for things. "Mobile payments have become so common in China that paying with cash is practically unheard-of, even with street performers and taxi drivers."[43] One mobile payment service in China, Alipay, has over 900 million users. As more and more people are paying for things via automated payments, it makes sense that churches also have a system for automated giving. A survey of over one thousand churches found that "the ability to accept automatic, recurring donations" was the most important factor shared by financially healthy churches.[44]

## Environment

Here's a bit of what's happened on our planet in terms of the environment over the past few years:

- "Of China's 560 million urban residents, only one percent breathe air considered safe by European Union standards."[45]

- Over 1 billion people do not have daily access to clean drinking water.[46]

- "Every year, 8 million metric tons of plastics enter" our oceans—the equivalent of "dumping one New York City garbage truck full of plastic into the ocean every minute of every day for an entire year."[47]

- The last four years have been the four hottest years since the National Oceanic and Atmospheric Administration (NOAA) began keeping records 139 years ago.[48]

- Sea levels have risen by 8 inches since 1880, and 3.7 inches since 1995.[49]

We may disagree on the causes of all of the above, but we should be able to agree that we can take actions to make things better for us and coming generations. We think it is safe to say we really are grateful that some passionate group of individuals worked to pass the Clean Air Act of 1970. Because of these generous folks, smog has all but disappeared in the United States. The San Francisco Bay Area has pristine blue sky, and people can now actually see the mountains east of Los Angeles. Rivers that once caught fire in Ohio are again teeming with fish. Gone also are acid rain and fluorocarbons. Aren't we glad people in the past did things to make life better for us today? The limitations and cost of fossil fuels have also driven innovation in the auto industry, resulting in hybrids and electric vehicles that can go hundreds of miles for just a few dollars.

It seems that in spite of a growing scientific consensus that human activity and fossil fuels are at least partly responsible for disappearing ice caps and rising sea levels, many Christians take a stand *against* such findings simply because the findings are supported by scientists (or movie stars or an opposing politician or some other group). Whereas in the past, Christians were often at the forefront of science, believing they were discovering, through their research, the very manner, mind, and methods of God, scientific evidence, for some believers, is rejected simply because it comes from the field of science. Are we alienating the scientific community and the younger generation by clinging to stubborn provincial views? Are these people thinking, "How can I believe what this person says about God and the unseen world when they reject the evidence of the seen world?"

How we view our care for the environment will also greatly affect how millennials and Gen Z view the church. A 2018 study by Gallup revealed that 67 percent of people aged eighteen to twenty-nine and 49 percent of those aged thirty to forty-nine say global warming is real, human-made, and a serious threat.[50] *Time* magazine's 2019 "Person of the Year" was sixteen-year-old Swedish climate activist Greta Thunberg, who is mobilizing her generation around climate change issues.

For the sake of the gospel, would it be so radical for a church to have its own recycling center or administer a neighborhood carpool to get to church? Would it be that out of the ordinary? We can't do everything but all of us can do something. On a day like today, what might we be doing to honor the proclamation that "the earth is the Lord's and everything in it" (Ps 24:1).

## Politics

What are the political forces that are shaping our world today? Communism, as a political and social reality, no longer poses the political and military threat of yesterday. The largest country that still lives under the political banner of communism, China, has abandoned the economic principles of Marx and embraced a quasi–free-market economy. And since the terrorist attacks of September 11, 2001, the United States has changed its tactics and position in world politics, not only going after terrorists but also engaging the countries that support them. In past generations, our battle was to stop the spread of communism. Today, American policy is to spread freedom and democracy around the globe.

In the United States, politics have become increasingly divisive for many. Those on the other side of the aisle are seen not just as different or wrong but as evil. Politics and faith have made unlikely, blanket-hogging bedfellows. The perception that evangelicals embrace a particular political party is not entirely inaccurate. More than 81 percent of white evangelicals voted for Trump in the 2016 presidential election.[51] In 2012, 78 percent of white evangelicals voted for Romney. The 2008 election exit polls were not much different, with 74 percent of evangelicals casting votes for McCain.[52]

Recently, a friend of mine (Eric's) was engaged in a conversation with a young Jewish woman who was investigating Christianity. Her main hesitation was expressed in her sincere question: "If I become a Christian, do I have to become a Republican?" The moral high ground is not a political platform but the word of God. *Sojourners* editor Jim Wallis writes, "Endorsing political candidates is a fine thing, but ordaining them is not."[53] If it's true that, as various writers have said, "we are not voting for a pastor but a president," then let's be sure we don't ordain them as "God's leader." To reach a multicultural generation with the gospel is going to take some serious rethinking about the melding of faith and politics. The danger of affiliating too closely with any political party is that we can no longer judge that party's actions by the values of the kingdom of God—by which all political systems must be judged. Let's not forget that in Roman times, "to the populace all religions were equally true; to the philosophers all were equally false; and to the politicians all were equally useful."[54] So let's just be diligent about being a pawn in someone else's strategy.

## Religion

Back in the seventies, I (Eric) was a deacon in a Baptist church in San Diego. Now imagine this: A family would visit the church on Sunday morning, fill out a visitor's card, and expect a visit from some church folk on Wednesday evening and would have pie and coffee waiting. We'd pass out a little brochure on the church and then pass out *The Four Spiritual Laws* and introduce this gospel presentation with "And this is the foundation of what we believe it is to be a Christian." It was not unusual for the entire family to trust Christ and show up the following Sunday for baptism. And we thought this was tough ministry and spiritual warfare! In America those days are gone.

If those days are gone, what kind of day is today? In January 2019, to establish an authentic baseline on the state of the church, LifeWay Research surveyed one thousand Protestant churches of all sizes and discovered the following (parentheses ours):[55]

- Six in ten Protestant churches are plateaued or declining in attendance. (But that also means that 40 percent are growing.)

- More than half (54 percent) saw fewer than ten people become new Christians in the past twelve months. (But that also means that half saw more than ten people become new Christians.)

- 57 percent have fewer than 100 people attending each week.

- 21 percent average fewer than 50.

- 11 percent average more than 250 for their worship services.

- 44 percent have one or fewer full-time staff members.

- 3 percent of churches added a multisite. (If there are ~350,000 churches in America, this represents 10,500 churches that added a multisite. Even if these numbers are cut in half, that is still a lot of multisite churches being added.)

- 12 percent indicated they were involved in opening a new church. (This percentage would indicate that 42,000 churches are involved in church planting. Again, if these are exaggerated by a factor of five, that would still mean over 8,000 churches being started each year.)

That's the state of the church, but there is more to the story. Pew and Barna research reveals that millennials and the generation that follows them (Gen Z) have less interest in church than previous generations. Sixty-four percent of millennials raised in the church have dropped out,[56] but we go about like business as usual. Albert Einstein is often mistakenly cited as the source of what is nonetheless a wise adage, that "doing the same thing over and over again and expecting a different result" is the definition of insanity. Doing the same thing over and over again *with prayer* and expecting a different result may be the definition of Christian insanity. Without going into all the data from Barna or Pew, what millennials and those who follow them want in a church is different than what previous generations wanted in their church experience. And they are not unusual in what they want. Every generation seems to believe that they have a more authentic faith than their parents or grandparents. Perhaps what millennials are looking for was coherently expressed in the words of the late Rachel Held Evans. In 2013, at age thirty-two, she wrote:

> What millennials really want from the church is not a change in style but a change in substance. We want an end to the culture wars. We want a truce between science and faith. We want to be known for what we stand for, not what we are against. We want to ask questions that don't have predetermined answers. We want churches that emphasize an allegiance to the kingdom of God over an allegiance to a single political party or a single nation. We want our LGBT friends to feel truly welcome in our faith communities. We want to be challenged to live lives of holiness, not only when it comes to sex, but also when it comes to living simply, caring for the poor and oppressed, pursuing reconciliation, engaging in creation care and becoming peacemakers. You can't hand us a latte and then go about business as usual and expect us to stick around. We're not leaving the church because we don't find the cool factor there; we're leaving the church because we don't find Jesus there. Like every generation before ours and every generation after, deep down, we long for Jesus. . . . I would encourage church leaders eager to win millennials back to sit down and really talk with them about what they're looking for and what they would like to contribute to a faith community. Their answers might surprise you.[57]

For the immediate future, we sense that following Jesus will be a greater magnet than ascribing to prescribed doctrinal tenets. Though researchers tend to focus on what's wrong with millennials and Gen Z, there are many outliers creating a different and more hopeful story. The 2020 Passion Conference focusing on eighteen- to twenty-five-year-olds gathered more than 65,000 millennials and Gen Z-ers for worship, teaching, service, and mission in the Mercedes-Benz stadium in Atlanta. Our friend Grant Skeldon, author of *The Passion Generation: The Seemingly Reckless, Definitely Disruptive, but Far from Hopeless Millennials*, offers some insight into what millennials want.

The church has called millennials to join the church. Millennials however want to *be* the church. What do I mean? The church wants millennials to show up on Sunday, volunteer where we can, and tithe—just like our parents and grandparents did. But that bar is too low. It's not compelling. There's this idea that millennials will leave the church if we call them to do too much. Well, I think they're leaving the church because we call them to do too little. The world is giving bigger responsibilities than the church. Today if a young person joins the military, they are entrusted with a lethal weapon on foreign soil. . . . If a young person joins the church, they are placed on the parking team, the greeting team or the children's ministry. The world is saying "Let's go, right now." The church is saying, "Slow down, just wait." I think the church is the right place with the wrong urgency and the world is the wrong place with the right urgency.[58]

Each year, through his nonprofit, Initiative Network (initiativenetwork.org), Grant and his small team gather scores of millennial and Gen Z leaders from ministry, arts and entertainment, business, and other fields who are using their talents to influence tens of millions in their generation who follow them live or through social media. Grant's gentle admonition to baby boomers and Gen Xers is this: "If you're not discipling anyone, please refrain from criticizing the next generation."[59] That's a good word.

How and how often we gather is changing. There was a time when the faithful gathered at least three times per week—Sunday morning, Sunday evening, and Wednesday evening. Today if a believer is in church three times per month, they are considered an attendance rock star. When we ask pastors, "What do you think the church will be like in twenty years?" the answers are almost always the same: "Well, I know the church will be here. . . . I'm just not sure what it will look like."

Currently, 45 percent of Americans use the internet to access spiritual content.[60] Today thousands of churches live-stream their services around the world. This past year our friends at Connection Pointe Church in Indiana told us that a woman from Colorado had come to faith through being part of their online service and flew to Indianapolis to be baptized at Connection Pointe. Crossroads Cincinnati sees their online service as a stepping stone to real community by connecting online visitors to one another (with their permission, of course) within a geographic area.

In 2016 we (Rick and Eric) had breakfast with a virtual reality (VR) expert to talk about the possibilities of a VR church. The Oculus Rift VR headset had just been released, and after a short demo we both sensed that one day, VR churches would be inevitable for people who longed for deeper human connection in the digital space. Today VR churches have formed with thousands of "members" from dozens of countries coming together for community and spiritual growth.

## The Future of the Church

Our hunch is that online church or virtual church will continue to be a great supplement but not a great long-term substitute for most of God's flock. Vineyard Columbus (Ohio) pastor Rich Nathan recently tweeted, "People say, 'I get together with a few Christian friends. Isn't that church?' The answer is a resounding NO! The beauty of church is that WE don't get to pick the people, Christ does! He picks people who differ from us in every way. Then he commands us to LOVE them!"[61] It's very difficult for iron to sharpen iron online.

In June of 2015, Harvard professor Tyler J. VanderWeele presented a brief lecture titled "Religion and Health: New Empirical Research" as part of Harvard's Lectures That Last series. In this talk Dr. VanderWeele presented convincing data that showed that people who attend religious services once a week or more live dramatically longer than those who do not. He concludes his presentation by putting forth a possible cause for this longer life expectancy:

> For the roughly half of Americans who do already believe in God but do not regularly attend services, the research on health and attendance perhaps constitutes an invitation back to communal religious life. Something about the communal religious experience . . . seems to matter. Where else today does one find a community with the possibility of a shared moral and spiritual vision, a sense of moral accountability, where the essential task of the members is to love and care for one another. The teachings, the relationships, the spiritual practices, over time, week after week, taken together, gradually alters behavior, creates meaning, alleviates loneliness, and shapes a person in ways, perhaps, too diverse to document. Such things alter health.[62]

## We Live in a Liminal Time

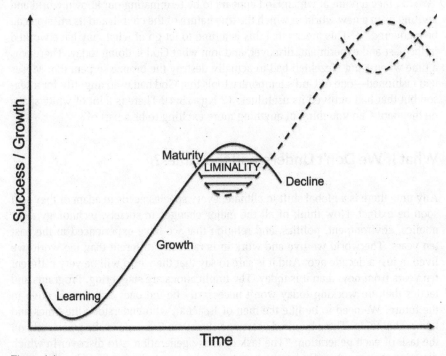

Figure 1.1

Perhaps we need to rethink the actual life-shaping benefits of analog attendance.

We also think that churches that do not have an external focus and a focus on discipleship will lack community credibility. Barna's research shows that "two of the most important ways to be positioned in the mind of the unchurched are first, as a ministry that regularly and effectively serves the needs of the poor, and second, as a church that understands young people and provides the kind of mentoring and development they need to thrive in life."[63]

In his book *Mission after Christendom*, David Smith suggests that we are currently living in a time of "liminality" (see figure 1.1), which he defines as a state between two cultural paradigms. In a liminal state, what used to work no longer works, but what will work has not yet been fully discovered. A liminal state describes preteen boys in tribal societies who are wrested from their mothers, are circumcised, and live together for a season with the men of the tribe across the river before their initiation into full manhood: no longer children but not yet men. Liminality describes the people of Israel when they were carried off into captivity, sitting by the rivers of Babylon. Everything they knew about connecting with God through a temple and a calendar back in Jerusalem no longer worked. How they would connect with God in a foreign land had not yet been discovered. But it would be discovered. In liminal times, there is confusion because the path is unclear, but the good news is we are not victims of a future state—we actually get to help create that future state. Missiologist Alan Roxburgh invites us to be part of the solution: "We . . . face a point at which God appears to be terminating our known world and inviting us to a new world in which the true nature of the church and its mission can be recovered."[64] This means that this is a time to let go of what may have worked in the past and experiment, discover, and join what God is doing today. There was a time when King Hezekiah had to actually destroy the bronze serpent that Moses had fashioned—one of God's temporary tools that God had used mightily for a season but that had outlived its usefulness (2 Kgs 18:4). There is a lot of white space on the map! Can you think of anything more exciting to be a part of?

## What If We Don't Understand the Times?

Any time there is a global shift in climate, every species needs to adapt or they will soon be extinct. Now think of all the major changes in society, technology, economics, environment, politics, and religion that we have experienced in the past ten years. The world we live and work in is radically different than the world we lived in just a decade ago. And it is safe to say that the world will be very different ten years from now than it is today. The implications are staggering. Programs and tactics that are working today won't necessarily be the ones that are effective in the future. We need to be like the men of Issachar, who understood the times and knew what to do. Three hundred years ago, Jonathan Edwards spoke presciently on the task of each generation: "The task of every generation is to discover in which direction the sovereign Redeemer is moving, then move in that direction."[65]

If the church is God's enterprise in the world, then we who are stewards, managers, and entrepreneurs in the enterprise need to be as discerning and as savvy as those in any other organization; indeed, given the stakes, we would argue that we should be even more so than in any other enterprise. The future will not be shaped by doing more or better or harder what we have done in the past. The key will be knowing what to embrace and release going forward.

Admittedly, looking at the church landscape, statistics show that many of us have been content to do what we have always done. We have not always understood how to act or react to this liminal state in which we find ourselves. We have confused method with message and have often been more concerned with maintaining what we are doing than with innovating new solutions to meet current and future needs in order to share the timeless message of Christ.

If we don't take time to understand and embrace today, we are left with only looking back, which often leads to self-preservation and maintenance. Even if we happen to be a church that has a lot of people, so much of our energy can be spent on simply attracting people and keeping them coming back. We have to ask ourselves not "What kind of day was yesterday?" but "What kind of day is today?"

## The Leadership Challenge

We feel that this book will be of benefit to every Christ-follower, but it is usually leaders who have the ability to bring about the changes needed to bring the future into the present. The Leadership Challenge presented at the end of each chapter broadens the scope of application of the chapter from the individual to the church or organization. It is our hope that this feature will bring forth insights and questions to help you lead the externally focused journey.

- What deep changes have you experienced in society, technology, economics, environment, politics, religion, and your own organization in the past five to ten years?

- What do you expect the future will be like in the next five to ten years in these same areas?

- How should these changes influence missional living?

- Where is most of your energy currently going?

- Who gives you insight and provides glimpses of future vision and timely understanding?

# 2.

## Focus: They Choose the Window Seat, Not the Aisle Seat

*Calls command that you attach yourself to something infinite and lasting so you can escape the life you thought you deserved and replace it with the life you were meant for.*

—John P. Schuster, *Answering Your Call*[1]

Both of us have logged a lot of miles sitting on airplanes. A few years ago I (Eric) passed two million miles on United Airlines, and Rick has traveled more than I have. Our work and friendship have led to some great adventures traveling together. We've been able to observe and participate in the work of God, and see a few sights along the way, all over the United States and Asia. That means a lot of time sitting on planes, and we know firsthand what a good seat looks and feels like.

### Seat 24E

As frequent flyers we get to know the best seats on the plane. We've noticed that if we can get the bulkhead seats right behind the first-class section and stick our feet under the divider, into the first-class section, our feet feel more refreshed when we arrive at our destination. We don't know why, but that's the way it works.

Arguably, the worst seat on an airplane is the non-reclining middle seat in the very back row, in front of the galley and across from the lavatory. On an Airbus A319, this seat is 24E—the middle seat in the last row. The seat is stiff, stubbornly refusing to recline. One time, while flying from Denver to Dallas, I was in row 23 and behind me were two federal officers with a handcuffed prisoner sitting between them in seat 24E—cruel and unusual punishment. Seat 24E is usually the last seat to be sold, and for good reason. The passengers in row 24 are the last to get beverage service and the last to deplane.

Middle seats, in general, are not good seats. So that leaves us with two other seat choices—the window seat and the aisle seat. Arguably, the best seat on an airplane is an aisle seat. For legroom and comfort there is nothing like an aisle seat in an airplane. From the aisle seat you can actually get up and move around the plane when the seatbelt sign is turned off. You can access your luggage in the overhead compartment with ease. You can see the drink cart coming down the aisle and ask

19

for refills or another bag of pretzels without having to shout. From the aisle seat you can do almost everything more conveniently than you can from the window seat except one thing: look out the window. And looking out the window may be the most important thing you can do if you want to know what's going on outside the plane.

We can think of churches also as either "aisle-seat churches"—almost exclusively captured by what is happening inside the four walls of the church —or "window-seat churches"—those churches whose focus is external to the church and whose vision extends far beyond the four walls. If you want to be the best church *in* the community, choose the aisle seat (in first class, if you can), but if you want to be the best church *for* the community, slide over to the window seat.

## Attractional and Missional Churches

In Matthew 22:2–5, Jesus gives a kingdom parable to describe the external focus of window-seat churches that also describes the process of building the kingdom. Jesus chooses his words carefully and deliberately. This is about a king who invites friends and neighbors to his own son's wedding reception.

> The kingdom of heaven is like a king who prepared a wedding banquet for his son. He sent his servants to those who had been invited to the banquet to tell them *to come*, but they refused *to come*. Then he sent some more servants and said, "Tell those who have been invited that I have prepared my dinner: My oxen and fattened cattle have been butchered, and everything is ready. *Come to* the wedding banquet." But they paid no attention and went off—one to his field, another to his business.

Luke's account adds:

> But they all alike began to make excuses. The first said, "I have just bought a field, and I must go and see it. Please excuse me." Another said, "I have just bought five yoke of oxen, and I'm on my way to try them out. Please excuse me." Still another said, "I just got married, so I can't come." (Luke 14:18–20)

This parable describes the conundrum of what some refer to as an "attractional church." The attractional church is one that through its presence, programming, and marketing—everything from cool websites to four-color brochures to word-of-mouth to Facebook ads—seeks to attract people to its services. But like the busy people in the parable, many, many people "pay no attention" or "make excuses" as to why they cannot come to the banquet. Even a second attempt at describing the sumptuous meal did little to attract these busy people. It is like saying, "Look what we have on the menu. We've brought in a cadre of Michelin five-star chefs, and they are preparing their finest dishes. Won't you come?" If the finest food and a hand-delivered invitation can't fill the banquet hall, what chance do pastors have trying to persuade the community with their menu of relevant teaching, inspiring worship, a great youth ministry, fabulous facilities, and so on?

The operative words in the attractional model are "come to." In the attractional model, we are asking people to substitute something *we* think is valuable and important for something *they* think is valuable and important. We don't know what happens on Sunday mornings in your community, but in our Colorado community, Sunday mornings are prime time for youth sports or just plain downtime. Families are off skiing or snowboarding or taking a summer hike or a drive in the Rockies. I (Eric) even say, only half-jokingly, that perhaps we should advertise like this: "Church: for those uncreative individuals with nothing better to do on a Sunday morning." In essence, what Jesus is saying is that even if the king himself invites people to his own son's wedding reception where the finest of foods are served, a great many people will still not come. If people don't show up because of the host or the quality of the cuisine, what chance do *we* have? The inadequacy of being an attractional church is that the banquet hall is far from full. If you are merely an attractional church, most likely you are already approaching the limit of all you are able to attract to your church. Yet your banquet hall is far from full. Fortunately for the king, his criterion of success was not "Has everyone been invited?" or "Does everyone know what time the banquet is?" or "Does everyone know what we have on the menu?" but rather "Is my banquet hall full?"

Because the banquet hall was not full, the parable has a second component that reveals a second strategy. The king augments his "come to" strategy with a "go to" or "go out" strategy: *"Go to* the street corners" (Matthew 22:9), *"Go out . . . into the streets and alleys of the town. . . . Go out* to the roads and country lanes . . . *so that* my house will be full" (Luke 14:21, 23). The attractional church is a "come to" church. Externally focused churches can best be described as "go to" churches or sometimes as "missional" churches. These churches think of incarnation as much as they think of invitation. The good news is that you don't have to sacrifice one strategy to employ the other. You should want your church to become the best attractional church it can be. When people come to your church, there should be a full fare of what they can partake in. They should leave mumbling the words of the queen of Sheba and singing the church's praises: "'The report I heard . . . about your achievements and wisdom is true. . . . Indeed, not even half was told me'" (1 Kgs 10:6–7). "The teaching is very practical, my teens love the youth group, and I can hardly pull my kids away from Sunday school." People should be surprised by the excellence and authenticity of what your church offers, but simply recognize this: you are not reaching all you could be reaching by a "come to" strategy alone. You can also extend your reach into the community as far as you can through your "go to" model—employing those in your church to *go into* the highways and hedges of your community. This is what window-seat churches do. We find ourselves telling pastors wherever we go, "The only thing more difficult than getting the church to go into the community is getting the community into the church." It is actually far easier, through regular influence, to get the church into the community than to try through sporadic contact to get the community into the church.

## The Early Church: A Window-Seat Church

The life and teachings of Jesus Christ were profound, holistic, and transformational. His threefold ministry encompassed teaching, preaching, and healing (Matt 4:23; 9:35). To walk as his disciple, one was to "be merciful just as [God] is merciful" (Luke 6:36), love as Jesus loved (John 13:34–35), and be a neighbor to all in need (Luke 10:29–37). In the early centuries of the church, the Christ-followers, through their compassion and kindness, served the people around them, resulting in an estimated 40 percent growth per decade of the early church.[2] David Bosch's research on the expansion of the early church pieces together "a remarkable picture of the early Christians' involvement with the poor, orphans, widows, the sick, mineworkers, prisoners, slaves, and travelers. 'The new language on the lips of Christians . . . was the language of love.' But it was more than a language; it was a thing of power and action: This was a 'social gospel' in the very best sense of the word and was practiced not as a stratagem to lure outsiders to the church but simply as a natural expression of faith in Christ."[3]

Throughout the following centuries, the church played a major role in meeting social needs and curing social ills. Christians were at the forefront in the abolition of slavery, the enactment of child labor laws, and the establishment of public schools, universities, orphanages, and hospitals. Christian leaders like William Booth and Jane Addams led the way in restoring the bodies and minds, as well as the souls, of those who were converted. The Catholic scholar Thomas Massaro writes of the social impact the church has had throughout the centuries:

> Many of the laudable social institutions and practices that we take for granted today have their roots in teachings and activities of the Christian community, including the Catholic Church. For example, the complex system of hospitals and modern health care from which we all benefit sprang from charitable works that were sponsored by churches, both Protestant and Catholic, in previous centuries. Modern labor unions and group insurance policies are an outgrowth of various activities of guilds and sodalities, agencies through which members of the medieval church practiced mutual support, often under direct religious auspices. Churches organized the first schools in our nation and in other lands, and much of our educational system at all levels is still religiously affiliated. It was the church that cared for poor families before there were public social service agencies. The contemporary social work and nursing professions grew out of the efforts of church personnel, largely nuns, and laywomen, Catholic and Protestant alike, to assist families in need of resources, expertise and healing. For good reason, then, the church has been called the "godmother of the nonprofit sector."[4]

## Reasons the Church Is Not Engaged

Is this the kind of impact the church is experiencing today? For most churches, this transformational role has all but disappeared. One pastor noted, "The normal Christian life has become so sub-normal that the normal Christian looks abnormal."[5] An Oregon pastor recently commented, "Service has always been the DNA of Christianity, but for most people, it is a recessive gene in the gene pool." Why has much of the church withdrawn, either physically or psychologically, from the community that God has placed it in? We believe there are four factors that have influenced the withdrawal of the church from the community. These factors are missional, theological, secular, and personal.

## The Missional Factor

First there is the missional factor. Dr. Ram Cnaan, director of the Program for Religion and Social Policy Research at the University of Pennsylvania, writes:

> While religious organizations—the Church with a capital C—[have] sponsored many social programs throughout the world, congregations have historically been reluctant to become involved in social programs. After all, the primary mission of a congregation is to provide a religious framework and communal site for worshiping. Its second mission is to sustain the congregation and to guarantee resources sufficient to carry out its primary mission. Social services delivery can come only after these two missions are achieved.[6]

Cnaan defines the practical pressure that keeps churches buckled in their aisle seats. Congregational leaders ask, as leaders from our own churches have asked from time to time, "How can we meet all the needs 'out there' when we have so many needs right here in our church? First, let's meet the needs within the church, and then we will have greater capacity to meet the needs 'out there.'" In early 2006, the researcher Thom S. Rainer wrote, "In a recent survey of churches across America, we found that nearly 95% of the churches' ministries were for members alone. Indeed, many churches had no ministries for those outside the congregation."[7]

In early 2007, the findings from a study conducted for *Facts & Trends* were released to the public. The study was the result of an extensive survey conducted in all fifty states among a representative sample of 811 Protestant church senior ministers. The survey revealed:

- 39 percent are not highly interested in offering more programs for the community, saying:
  - they would rather focus on spiritual needs than on physical needs,
  - they would rather focus on their own congregation than on the community, . . .
  - their congregation . . . really isn't interested in community outreach.

This is fairly consistent across all major denominational groups . . . , as well as between evangelical and mainline churches.[8]

The "mission" of the church cannot merely be to maintain itself. Jesus never commanded the church to merely survive.

A few years ago, I (Eric) received the following email from an associate pastor that explains the difficulty of moving from the aisle seat to the window seat.

Eric,

So here I sit at Starbucks . . . yeah, I think I hate this place today. Listening to Wayne Newton so stop trying to push that on me. But that's not why I am writing. I have been involved in this whole externally focused church idea and thoughts for a while. Your article about paradigm shifts[9] put on paper some thoughts that have been stirring in me for about three years or so. As I drove around my community, I was saddened by two very crazy thoughts: how come there are so many needs, and why are there so many churches being built, yet the community is unchanged?

So all these thoughts led me to get fired from my position as an associate pastor—probably for the best anyway. I approached the church with applicable ways to integrate more into our community instead of trying to invite everyone to the church (which doesn't make sense to me anyway). So, I suggested little ways to make a Sunday church more passionate and directed to community transformation. That truly is my passion—to see community changed regardless of what happens to the church growth numerically. I proposed simple suggestions: What if we asked each small group to own a neighborhood in the community and twice a year serve them somehow? They could throw a block party, provide a day out through free child care, a physical service project, invite a person to talk on safety issues . . . whatever, just something small to get their feet wet . . . just trying to get them to think differently. I suggested that when we do events, we think them through differently. For example, why don't we invite children to the church for a movie night? What if we worked with the mothers' group in the community and plan a movie night at the park and then give the mothers' group the credit for pulling it off? What if we did a capital campaign to pay the homeowners' association fees for the single parents? These were just little ideas, but they led to a huge problem. It was not about the church then!

So, I kept gently trying to be a visionary and lead by example. I gathered a small group of people, and we began. After fourteen years of ministry, you would have thought I would have learned how to be institutionalized. Nope . . . haven't learned that yet. So, after fourteen years, I got the boot and was shown the door. Exact quote: "We are about the Sunday service and growing in worship." So I just wanted to say thanks for getting me fired. No, just kidding. It's cool and I trust God for what is next. I know my passion to see community changed and for churches to get it. I am totally in love with Jesus and I know he gets it.

Thanks man,

A Once and Future Associate Pastor

It's heartbreaking to read a story like that, but the pushback is often all too real.

## Theological Factors

A second issue is theological. Beginning with the Reformation, many believers wanted to separate themselves from the corrupt practices of the established church and state. There could be no cooperation, capitulation, or collaboration with Christians who were less dedicated and set apart than they themselves hoped for. The Swiss Brethren Anabaptists, for example, came up with seven areas of common agreement, among which was Article IV, titled "Separation from the Abomination," in the Schleitheim Confession of 1527:

> We are agreed . . . on separation: A separation shall be made from the evil and from the wickedness which the devil planted in the world; in this manner, simply that we shall not have fellowship with them (the wicked) and not run with them in the multitude of their abominations. This is the way it is: since all who do not walk in the obedience of faith, and have not united themselves with God so that they wish to do His will, are a great abomination before God, it is not possible for anything to grow or issue from them except abominable things. For truly all creatures are in but two classes, good and bad, believing and unbelieving, darkness and light, the world and those who (have come) out of the world, God's temple and idols, Christ and Belial; and none can have part with the other. . . .
>
> He further admonishes us to withdraw from Babylon and earthly Egypt that we may not be partakers of the pain and suffering which the Lord will bring upon them.[10]

Often Christians of this same ilk will quote verses like 2 Corinthians 6:17: "Wherefore come out from among them, and be ye separate, saith the Lord" (almost always quoted in the King James Version). But we firmly believe that this separation is a separation of values and life choices and not a separation of geography, since one cannot be salt, light, and leaven at a distance. These transformational agents work only when they actively mix with what needs to be changed.

Sometimes theological trends shape behavior. Toward the end of the nineteenth century, the eschatological teaching of premillennialism became a prominent popular theology of the day. A tenet of premillennialism is the imminent return of Jesus Christ, followed by a thousand-year reign of Christ on earth. A prerequisite to Christ's return was the preaching of the gospel to the entire world "as a testimony to all nations, and then the end [would] come" (Matt 24:14). It was this conviction that helped fuel the great missionary efforts of the late nineteenth and early twentieth centuries. An aberration of this teaching, however, was the notion that any effort Christians expended trying to make this world a better, more livable place, as opposed to getting people into heaven, was to *hinder and delay* the return of Jesus Christ. It was this attitude that exempted the church from engaging with the ills and hurts of the community. This theological stance, which set itself against amillennialists, who don't accept a literal thousand-year reign of Jesus, was the beginning of what church historian David Bosch refers to as the "great reversal,"[11] when most of the evangelical church, as it came to be called, exempted itself from involvement in societal ills.

## Secular Factors

The third reason churches have refrained from social ministry is because of the secularization of social services. Although it can be argued that the fount of human services is the church, little by little the church has both relinquished this role and been eased out of it by government and human service agencies—the "professionals." The late Diana Garland, writing in *Christianity and Social Work*, notes that secularization is not without effect: "'The spontaneous will to serve,' so evident in earlier church volunteers, was subverted by the drive for professionalization. Previous values that had stressed compassion, emotional involvement, and vigorous love of humanity . . . were 'educated out' in preference for a 'scientific trained intelligence and skillful application of technique.'"[12] Average congregants often feel underqualified to engage the homeless, immigrants, orphans, widows, and others in need when so much expertise seems to be required.

The church is often absent from the conversation regarding societal ills and social needs. A few years ago, both of us were sitting in a meeting with some city officials looking over a publication titled *Quality of Life in Boulder County: A Community Indicators Report*.[13] In this report, there was not a single reference to churches being part of the solution in addressing the top community needs such as at-risk youth, health care, and homelessness, although "public agencies," "businesses," and "nonprofit agencies" were frequently cited. Addressing the absence of religion-based literature in social services, Ram Cnaan reports that in a review of more than 35,000 abstracts of articles for social workers published between 1977 and 1997, only 220 mentioned the term *religion*. Further analysis failed to identify a single source that dealt with a religion-based social service organization as a service provider or partner for social work. Nor was there any mention of religion-based social services that complement the services provided by the state, foundations, residents' associations, and academic disciplines.[14]

Cnaan further notes that similar patterns were found in papers presented at academic conferences, in textbooks, in course outlines, and in encyclopedias of social work. Surely an aisle-seat church that focuses primarily on itself is not the church that Jesus came to build. Believers are called to be salt and light (Matt 5:13–14), not for and to themselves but for and to the world around them.

A few years ago, an editorial appeared in Canada's *Vancouver Sun* newspaper regarding Tenth Avenue Alliance Church's ministry to the homeless. The church "runs a daily drop-in service for people, some of whom are homeless, as well as an Out of the Cold program that provides overnight accommodation for homeless people."[15] The city demanded that the church obtain a social services permit because its ministry to the homeless didn't qualify as "church use." We can hardly blame the city for such a misconception when we as the church have been content to sing, pray, and take notes within the confines of the four walls.

## Personal Factors

Sometimes we want to stay in the aisle seat because venturing to the window seat and engaging in what we find is just too hard, even when we are in ministry. A while back, I (Eric) received this email from a good friend, Ian Vickers, who is committed to serving people on the margins. He's far from tossing in the towel, but the conflicted emotions are all too real.

Hello Eric,

I thought about you today as I was reviewing some of my week. Monday was a day filled with interesting emotional highs and lows. At 8:30 a.m. I tried to help a homeless guy out, but it did not go so well. He ended up calling me a "#@%&* pastor" for not helping more. After he was done, I realized that a wristband on his arm was from one of the local hospitals. Well, I offered to take him to a place where he could get some help and then to pray for him. He said, "I don't need any #@%&* prayer. I am going to sue this #@%&* church." Yeah, he was one frustrated guy. I still prayed for him but struggled to see Jesus in disguise through this event.

## A Timely Look at the Scriptures

A while back I (Eric) asked Rich Nathan, lead pastor of Vineyard Church in Columbus, Ohio, to lead a devotional for a group of pastors I had pulled together with Leadership Network. Rich's insights on why churches don't engage with broken people outside the church were cogent and powerful. Rich began by reminding us of the two grandest parables in the Gospel of Luke—the prodigal son (Luke 15) and the good Samaritan (Luke 10). In the case of the prodigal, this younger son was a victim of his own personal rebellious sin. No one duped or coerced him into his circumstances. He willingly, consciously, and deliberately walked away from his family to pursue a lifestyle of partying, drunkenness, and licentiousness. He is today's drug addict or alcoholic or teenage single mom. Rich points out that in cases like that of the prodigal son, God rescues people through forgiveness, and we often do not realize just how far God's forgiveness extends. So, we stand in the background with our arms folded like the older brother, wanting nothing to do with helping this poor-choosing individual. After all, we wouldn't want to enable a person to the point of codependency. Our problem is that we don't understand grace. God rescues through forgiveness. The good news of the gospel is that no matter what you've done, you can turn to God and be forgiven, and it sounds too good to be true.

In the parable of the good Samaritan, the injured man was not a victim of his own personal sin but rather of being sinned against—social sin. There was the victim, beaten and robbed of everything he had and left for dead on the side of the road. But look! Hope is on the way in the form of God's people—the priest and the Levite. But no, they pass by on the other side of the road. Most likely they were on their way to Jerusalem and had sacred or spiritual duties to perform, and must not the spiritual take precedence over the physical? Others can mend the physical body, but only God's people can carry out God's work. Right? What good is it to send well-fed people to hell? We've got to care for the souls of people. Most often we don't engage in healing the hurts because at the end of the day, we are twenty-first-century Gnostics. We value the immaterial and eternal to the exclusion of the physical and temporal. We are resistant to a gospel that has social implications. We'll leave that to others. So as both parables point out, we cleverly devise an apologetic for disengagement. The first parable calls us to evangelism—to extend grace and forgiveness to the most unworthy. The second parable calls us to engagement in social action—charity, mercy, and justice. And this two-fisted gospel must be big enough that we can wrap both arms around a hurting world.

Writing with tongue in cheek, Atlanta's Robert Lupton, in his wonderful little book *Theirs Is the Kingdom*, expounds:

> People with a heart to serve others want to know that their gifts are invested wisely. At least I do. I don't want my alms squandered by the irresponsible and the ungrateful. And since I'm often in a position to determine who will or will not receive assistance, I've attempted to establish criteria to judge the worthiness of potential recipients.
>
> [The following list is truncated and bulleted for convenience.]
>
> - A truly worthy poor woman is a widow over sixty-five living alone without family.
> - A truly worthy poor young man is out of school, unemployed, but not living off his mother.
> - A truly worthy poor young woman has illegitimate children conceived prior to Christian conversion and is now celibate.
> - A truly worthy poor family is devout, close-knit, has a responsible father working long hours at minimum wage wherever he can find work.
>
> I want to serve truly worthy poor people. The problem is they are hard to find. Someone on our staff thought he remembered seeing one back in '76 but can't remember for sure.[16]

## Focus

Where is the focus of our church? Is it inside or outside the church? Aisle churches think a lot about internal programs—activities that meet the needs of those inside the church. At the end of the day, the church has been reduced to a warehouse of religious goods and services. Aisle churches "count nickels and noses" (or "bucks and butts," depending on your denominational preference) as a measure of their effectiveness. Churches that choose the window seat think that church should be something more. Church is not merely caring for those you have but going after those you don't have. In his book *The Present Future*, our good friend Reggie McNeal writes:

> The target of most church ministry efforts has been on the church itself and church members. Just look at how the money is spent and what the church leadership spends time doing. We have already rehearsed the poor return on investment we are seeing for this focus. The church that wants to partner with God on his redemptive mission in the world has a very different target: the community. In the past, if a church had any resources left over after staffing Sunday school, and so on, then it went to the com-

munity. In the future, the church that "gets it" will staff to and spend its resources on strategies for community transformation.[17]

We like what Reggie says. When you look at the resources (time, finances, prayer, technology, and people), how much of those resources is expended outside the church?

## Blindness and the Nearsighted

Sometimes we just don't get it—until God intervenes. Do you remember when Peter was hanging out at Simon's beach house in Joppa (Acts 10:6)? Through a vision, God showed Peter that he needed to go to Caesarea and preach the gospel to a non-Jewish centurion and his family. Although the Hebrew Scriptures clearly foretold that Jesus was to be a blessing to all peoples (Gen 12:3, also explored by Paul in Eph 3:4–10), Peter and his Jewish brothers were "blind" to this truth. The author of the book of Acts takes two full chapters to tell Peter's story of converting the Gentiles and how the Jewish believers finally "got it" (Acts 11:18).

As human beings, we always suffer from some type of blindness. Look at the life of John Newton. On business trips, he would spend several hours praying and reading the Bible each morning, with another round of prayers at midday. As a ship captain, he enjoyed long spells of solitude on deck, keeping a diary and recording that he knew no "calling that . . . affords greater advantages to an awakened mind, for promoting the life of God in the soul."[18] His expensive cargo required extra officers and crew, reducing his onboard responsibilities. "I never knew sweeter or more frequent hours of divine communion, than in my last two voyages to Guinea, when I was either almost secluded from society on shipboard, or when on shore I have wandered through the woods reflecting on the singular goodness of the Lord to me."[19] John Newton recorded those words while transporting African slaves and having his savings invested in the slave ship business. "For more than thirty years after he left the slave trade, during which time Newton preached thousands of sermons, published half a dozen books, and wrote *Amazing Grace* and 279 other hymns, he said not a word in public against slavery."[20]

Newton was blind to what is now so obvious. Even though he penned the words "I once . . . was blind, but now I see," apparently he only had the ability to see things up close. He was nearsighted. When he truly became "sighted," he devoted the remainder of his life to speaking out and attempting to end the slave trade.

Blindness and nearsightedness are still prevalent today. At the HIV/AIDS Summit, Saddleback pastor Rick Warren narrated his own story of blindness. "I have two advanced theological degrees and have read the Bible cover to cover dozens of times. I don't know how I missed over twelve hundred verses on the poor and disenfranchised. How did I miss the biggest health crisis in history?"[21]

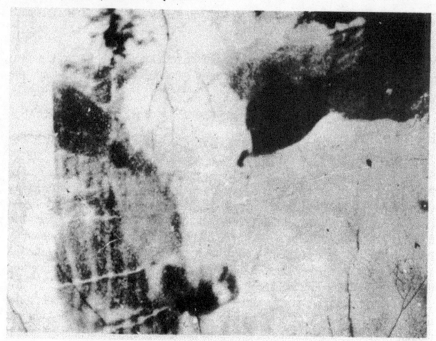

Figure 2.1

Sometimes when we speak, we ask everyone in the audience to stand up. Then we project a picture on the screen (see figure 2.1) and ask the people in the audience to sit down when they recognize the object. About half the people sit down immediately and find it hard to believe that people all around them are still standing. During the next minute, a few more utter, "Oh, I see it," and sit down. About 30 percent just stand there wondering what it is that they don't see. But once the object is pointed out, it is so obvious that you cannot *not* see it. From that point on, it is clear. We think it's the same with the orientation of a church. Once a church gets engaged outside the walls, it discovers that's really where the action is. Did you ever notice that every pilot flying a plane always has the window seat? If one is going to lead, one must do it from the window seat. You've got to look out the window.

## Turning Their Chairs Around

Hope Church is a large suburban church in Cordova, Tennessee, within a stone's throw of Memphis. Hope began in 1988 with a core group of twenty-five people and today has a weekly worship attendance of over seven thousand. Looking out the window has almost always been a part of Hope's DNA. Though the setting is suburban, the focus is urban. Each week, Hope sends over two hundred people to seven different sites around the city to help children increase their reading proficiency. Hope sponsors year-round food and clothing drives and provides coaches, equipment, and uniforms for inner-city youth baseball and softball programs as part of its RBI (Return Baseball to the Inner City) initiative. In 2001 the church created a separate 501(c)(3) organization called Oasis of Hope to partner with an impoverished neighborhood in North Memphis. Oasis has a vibrant ministry to seniors, a housing program that builds and rehabs homes, an appliance store that employs neighbors and provides low-cost appliances to the community, and a youth program that is impacting next-generation leaders. The church's "Scrubs Team"—a volunteer janitorial crew—saves $186,000 annually to put into missions. The church's kitchen ministry has an offering called Dinner on Demand, a program where members come to the church's kitchen to prepare wonderful meals to take home to their freezers. In the fourteen years of its existence, that program has raised over $2 million for missions. The director of urban ministries, Pastor Eli Morris, began attending Hope two months after it opened its doors and was the first staff member hired at Hope. The first week he was on the job, he was working side-by-side with members of Hope and members of the community building a house for a working-poor family in the inner city. Twice a year, Eli leads a four-day "urban plunge" into inner-city Memphis. Over the years, almost every leader at Hope has been a part of one of these missional forays into the city.

How does a church get such focus? Eli's heart was touched when he was student teaching at the toughest, poorest junior high school in Memphis while a student at Memphis State. "That's where my heart flipped. The teacher I was working under was a pastor who made his living as a history teacher. His influence on me radically transformed me."

Eli speaks to every class of new members that comes through the doors of Hope. As the group sits in a large circle, facing one another, Eli asks, "How much space is between us in this circle?" The answer is usually three hundred to four hundred square feet. Then Eli has everyone turn their chairs outward and asks, "How much space is outside the circle? What you see is the focus of Hope." Then Eli adds, "If you're coming to Hope to get all your needs met, you are in the wrong place. The 'story' is out there, not in the church." Eli is finding that the work the church performs is not only transforming the community but also transforming the people of Hope. "Our people have found that to spend oneself on the work of the gospel is the most refreshing experience in their faith walk," says Eli. "To come home tired and sore with blistered hands has proved to be their new definition of the gospel. The gospel has historically been a set of doctrines and theology, which of course it is, but the new definition for our people is the gospel in sweat and blood and relationship and tears—pouring out their lives into the lives of others."

Churches that transform communities are those that are inwardly strong but outwardly focused. An increasing number of churches are rediscovering their focus and thinking differently about what church should be. These are externally focused churches—window-seat churches that measure their effectiveness not by how many congregants are sitting in the pews but rather by how many congregants are engaged in the community. These are churches that firmly believe that if they are not engaged in meeting the needs of their communities, they are not the church that Jesus called them to be. Does your church take the window seat or the aisle seat?

## The Leadership Challenge

Changing seats is always difficult—especially if you've been buckled in the aisle seat for decades. Is it hard to become a window-seat church? Absolutely! But as we have opportunities to speak to pastors and Christian leaders around the world, we find ourselves saying, "As difficult as it is to get the church to go to the community, there is one thing even more difficult—getting the community to go to the church. As difficult as it is for the church to engage the community with words and works of love and grace, it is exponentially more difficult to try to entice the community into the church." Pastors and Christian leaders have the chance every week to influence the behavior and actions of the people who do come to church, but have very little influence on those who do not come to church. Where are you focusing your influence?

# 3.

# Purpose: They Practice Weight Training, Not Bodybuilding

*I'm not looking for an audience to fill up the church; I'm looking for an army to change the world.*

—Pastor Danny Carroll, Water of Life Community Church, Fontana, California

From the outside looking in, weight training and bodybuilding look nearly indistinguishable—presses, squats, thrusts, flies, pullovers, and curls. The ambient sounds of weight training and bodybuilding likewise are similar—the grunts and groans, the distinctive clang of the weights hitting the floor. But as much as these activities look and sound alike, they divide around *purpose*. Athletic records are continually being shattered largely because the strength and capacity of athletes is increasing thanks to weight training. Before the 1970s, training with weights was thought to make athletes "muscle-bound," so swimmers, golfers, and baseball players rarely, if ever, touched a barbell. To be competitive today, athletes must be training with weights. For athletes, weight training *is a means to a greater end*—to build strength, balance, and flexibility to go "faster, higher, stronger" in a given sport. Athletic records have fallen as swimmers, runners, baseball players, football players, and even golfers spend time in the weight room. Tiger Woods changed golf forever through his commitment to weight training, but he is hardly a bodybuilder. Athletes train for their event. Their training is not the event.

Bodybuilding is different. Bodybuilders train with weights for the sole purpose of making the body as muscular, beautiful, symmetrical, and physically imposing as possible. Quarts of oil, six-pack abs, a good tan, and a smile bigger than a swimsuit are all that are required to enter a bodybuilding contest. Churches that transform communities are those that build the body of Christ not to show off the size and strength of the body but to expand the capacity for ministry and service. They are internally strong but externally focused. The church is more like a training facility than a performance stage.

Bodybuilding churches that focus on themselves may very well be the most impressive and best churches *in* their communities, but it is the weight-training church that has the chance of being the best church *for* the community.

33

## Understanding Purpose

Understanding Ephesians 2:8–10 is pivotal in the theology of externally focused churches. Ephesians 2:8–9 tells us *how* we are saved—by grace through faith in Christ. Ephesians 2:10 tells us *why* God saved us—to do the good works that God prepared in advance for us to do. Every person who has experienced Ephesians 2:8–9 (that is, who has been saved by grace through faith) should, *by definition*, also be experiencing Ephesians 2:10—the good works God has prepared for them to do! We have not only a God-shaped vacuum in our lives but also a *purpose-shaped vacuum* in our lives. That God has prepared these good works beforehand implies that these good works are ours to discover, not invent.

Understanding this has dynamic implications for leaders. The leader's job then becomes nothing less than giving every person continued opportunities to discover their Ephesians 2:10 calling. A worthy goal would be for everyone who is a Christ-follower to be living out the good works God has created us to do. God has designed us to be his hands, feet, and voice in our world, and every major resource God gives us is given not just for personal experience but to make a difference in the world. Evangelistically, we believe that the more people are living out their Ephesians 2:10 calling, the more people will discover grace in their Ephesians 2:8–9 calling.

## God's Resources

Let's look at the resources God has given us to do those good works.

- Leaders to prepare us for good works

So Christ himself gave the apostles, the prophets, the evangelists, the pastors and teachers, to equip his people for works of service. (Eph 4:11–12)

God has not sent oil boys to grease us up for stage competition but gifted leaders to prepare us for service in the world. When the word of God is preached or taught, it is not just to help us feel better about ourselves but to equip us *"for every good work."* Missional thought leader Alan Roxburgh says, "The role of the pastor is shifting from one who tends to the hurts and needs of the congregation to one who teaches and trains the congregation to tend to the hurts and needs of the community."[1]

- The Scriptures to equip us for good works

All Scripture is God-breathed and is useful for teaching, rebuking, correcting and training in righteousness, so that the servant of God may be thoroughly equipped for every good work. (2 Tim 3:16–17)

God's Word is not a protein shake to add muscle mass; it is more of an energy bar that is useful in enabling us to do what we need to do today.

- The body to encourage us toward good works

And let us consider how we may spur one another on toward love and good deeds. (Heb 10:24)

God gives us like-minded friends to encourage us and spur us on toward making a difference. Spiritual friendships are a precious gift.

- Spiritual gifts to enable us to do good works

Each of you should use whatever gift you have received to serve others, as faithful stewards of God's grace in its various forms. (1 Pt 4:10)

God gives us spiritual gifts not to edify ourselves but rather to "serve others." The focus is outside ourselves, for the good of others.

- Resources to finance good deeds

Command those who are rich in this present world not to be arrogant nor to put their hope in wealth, which is so uncertain, but to put their hope in God, who richly provides us with everything for our enjoyment. Command them to do good, to be rich in good deeds, and to be generous and willing to share. (1 Tim 6:17–18)

Wealth is entrusted to us so that we have a greater capacity "to do good, to be rich in good deeds."

## Bringing It All Together

Here's the point: Every major resource God has given us—leaders to prepare us, the Word to equip us, the body to encourage us, spiritual gifts to enable us, and wealth to pay for things—points us toward *doing something* in this world. Once we really grasp this concept, ministry can be seen for what the Scriptures present it to be: an integral part of every Christ-follower's life. This is not bodybuilding. It is weight training.

# The Tipping Point of Growth

Each one of us instinctively seeks our own well-being in at least three areas. Using a truncated version of Abraham Maslow's "hierarchy of needs"[2] to illustrate our point, we contend that we seek first to have our basic physical needs met (see figure 3.1).

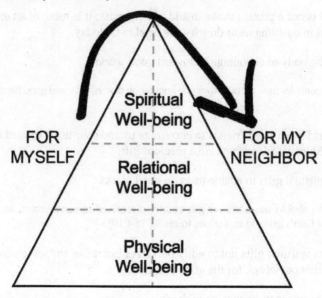

Figure 3.1

Physical needs are basic things like food, clothing, shelter, and security. We also structure our lives in such a way that our relationships with others are working. And last of all, we seek to be connected to God. To act purposefully to see that our physical, relational, and spiritual needs are met is the practical expression of what it means to love oneself. That makes sense.

But we don't truly grow until we begin loving, serving, and giving ourselves to someone *else*, someone beyond ourselves and even outside of friends and family. Loving those who love us comes as a natural expression of being part of the human family. Jesus pointed out that everybody does that, including "sinners" (Luke 6:31–35). Real spiritual growth occurs when the physical, relational, and spiritual well-being of our neighbor is *as important* as our own. This is what it means to "love our neighbor as ourselves," a crucial part of the Great Commandment (Matt 22:37–39). The theology that values the spiritual but not the physical comes from those who always have food in their stomach and slept in a warm bed last night.

## Real-Life Examples of Weight-Training Ministries

Let's look at a handful of ways externally focused church work is taking place in the world.

## Weight Training in Boulder

In the summer of 2008, three young women, aged nineteen to twenty-two, embarked on the adventure of their lives—to Africa. They had forged a friendship over the year. Sally was a regular customer at Buchanan's Coffee Pub, across from the University of Colorado, where Leah and Andrea served as baristas. They also connected in a small Bible study group at a nearby church. Leah and Andrea were going to Africa, and they invited Sally to go along. In Sally's words, "We had absolutely no idea what we were getting ourselves into; we only knew that we were ready!"[3] The three young women applied to go to Uganda through a non-sectarian service placement organization called Experiential Learning International (ELI; eliabroad.org), and after obtaining passports and getting the requisite immunizations, they were on their way to Africa. After landing in their city and taking a leisurely tour, they came across a decrepit under-resourced orphanage that was being closed by the government because of its awful condition. One of the women explains:

> It was a place that made your heart break. There were over 150 children living in a cramped four rooms with dirt floors and only a few doors, overflowing latrines, and absolutely no room for the kids to play. [The orphanage] was also a boarding school, but unfortunately there was an absence of electricity or windows and therefore some of the children had class in dark rooms while the others were taught outside in the blazing sun. The conditions were horrifying, and I feel that in order to fully understand, one has to go and witness it firsthand.... I fought back tears during my entire visit to the 150 vulnerable children. It is unthinkable to realize that these children are tucked away in an alley living lives in horrible conditions but all the while with huge smiles on their faces. We realized that something had to be done and that we were, no matter how unprepared we felt, the ones to do it.[4]

They would start a new orphanage that would be called Musana Children's Home. (*Musana* means "sunshine" in the local language.) Sally, Andrea, and Leah understood that God cared just as much for these little ones as for them, and they wanted to be the hands, feet, and voice of Jesus to each of these children. Sally and Leah have returned to Colorado to raise money for their new enterprise, while Andrea has stayed behind in Uganda to care for the children. On the plane ride home, Sally penned these words in her journal, copied from the book *Night*, written by Nobel Peace Prize winner and Holocaust survivor Elie Wiesel:

> There is much to be done, there is so much that can be done. One person . . . of integrity, can make a difference, a difference of life and death. As long as one dissident is in prison, our freedom will not be true. As long as one child is hungry, our lives will be filled with anguish and shame. What all these victims need above all is to know that they are not alone; that we are not forgetting them, that when their voices are stifled we shall lend them ours, that while their freedom depends on ours, the quality of our freedom depends on theirs.[5]

Now, over a decade later, Musana is thriving. Over four thousand students have been educated in the organization's three schools, resulting in a 300 percent increase in income for women. Musana employs over 280 workers, and over 40,000 people have received free medical service at its clinics. The annual budget of over $1 million is raised locally.

## Weight Training in Dallas

Bob Roberts of Northwood Church in Keller, Texas, ties spiritual growth and health to ministry and service. He puts it this way:

> I once believed that engaging the world and the poor was about helping them, but I've learned that serving humanity in the name of Jesus brings us far more than we give—it's the number one tool of discipleship in the world. If you truly want your church to be missional, put down your books, logs, and conferences, and touch the neediest people closest to you; then pick one spot in the world and engage however you can. You'll learn far more by doing than by reading.[6]

## Weight Training in Mexico City

My (Eric's) friend Craig Johring started going to Mexico in the late 1990s, leading campus summer mission projects with Cru (then Campus Crusade for Christ) on Mexican college campuses. As Craig's Spanish improved, he ventured beyond the campus, where he encountered really poor people living on the street or in sewers or the city dump, and began to invite others to join him in ministering to the poor. A few years ago, Craig joined forces with singer-songwriter and missionary Danny Leger and formed Hope of the Poor (hopeofthepoor.org). It's hard not to love their tagline, "Alleviating the poverty of being unloved," and their mission:

> We work with the poor. Our mission field is drug-addicted street kids, homeless families, and people who live at the city dump. We bring hope to the rejected, the lonely, and the unloved. We feed the poor, rent homes to take families off the street and work with employers to find them jobs. But we don't stop there. Mother Theresa [sic] often said the greatest poverty is being unloved. We want to inspire all generations to radically love and bring hope to the hopeless.[7]

In 2019 over 330 college students spent four to seven days with Craig on various "mission pilgrimages." At the end of each trip Craig challenges these students to go back to their cities and encounter the poor. Craig says, "With Hope of the Poor we step into the lives of people who are unloved, unwanted, and just value them as human beings. We find that the baseline thing we need to do is to show up in people's lives and love them for who they are and what they have to offer." By this simple act, families are taken off the street through permanent housing and a job; addicted, homeless street kids become clean and productive; children living in the dump are provided with shoes and uniforms so they can attend school. As Craig says, "Ninety to 95 percent of ministry is just showing up."

## Research

In 2006, the School of Social Work at Baylor University released the findings of its study of over 6,400 congregants from thirty-six congregations regarding the connection between service and faith. The study revealed at least two significant things:

1. Those who were personally involved in community ministry were not only more likely to volunteer time to help others, provide hospitality to strangers, and participate in activities promoting social justice, but also more likely to pray, attend worship service, and give financially to the church.

2. Although participating in community ministry once a week or more tended to be associated with higher scores on measures of faith, participating in worship [or] activities more frequently is *not* associated with higher scores on measures of faith.[8]

Clearly, growth and service go together.

Healthy churches and service also go together. Kevin Ford, president of TAG Consulting, administered the company's Transforming Church Index, a 110-question survey, tabulated from over 25,000 respondents. Here's what he concluded: "Nothing could have prepared me for the biggest surprise from our data. I had expected a slight gap between the two sets in 'members involved in ministry,' but what we found more closely resembled a canyon: Among healthy churches, 93 percent of members considered themselves to be involved in some form of ministry (though not necessarily at their church), compared to only 11 percent of members in the less healthy churches."[9]

No doubt about it: a healthy church is a serving church, and a serving church is a healthy church. Without service, we become like the would-be marathoner who is always carbo-loading but never racing.

### Building Capacity in Young People

Another 2006 study by Baylor University's School of Social Work indicates that the best way to build and strengthen the faith of young people is not through the church service but through community service. The study of more than six hundred adolescents from thirty-five Protestant congregations also revealed a few keys to effective service. First, it must be "authentic service that meets real human needs." Second, this service must be coupled with the opportunity to process the experience with adults. They want to serve alongside adults. Third, "young people need to be partners in ministry, not solely the object of ministry." This is an important and empowering distinction for developing new generations of spiritual leaders for today as well as tomorrow." One of the co-investigators, the late Diana Garland concludes the report by writing, "This should be a compelling argument for congregational leaders to be intentional about involving parents and youth together in community ministry programs. The opportunities to help our youth grow in their faith literally are as close as the neighborhoods outside the church's door."[10]

When teens serve alongside their parents as partners in ministry, they are living out a vital experience of what it means to be authentically Christian. Researchers Thom and Sam Rainer have come to similar conclusions:

> Many of our churches are producing a lot of soft and self-centered Christians. And the young people in our churches are getting the message. Churches that are outwardly focused are sending a different message. . . . That is the irony . . . the outwardly focused church creates better inwardly focused assimilation. As our young people meet the needs of others, they see that they are important to the life of the church, and thus they are prone not to enter the ranks of the dechurched.[11]

## Minimum Viable Spiritual Weight Training

For the past several years entrepreneurs have been launching businesses by starting with a "minimum viable product," or MVP. Wikipedia defines an MVP as "a product with just enough features to satisfy early customers and provide feedback for future product development."[12] So, in 1999 when Nick Swinmurn was thinking of starting an online shoe company, he tested the concept not by stocking a warehouse full of shoes, but taking pictures of shoes at a local shoe store, posting those pictures online, and then waiting for people to order those shoes. When orders came in, Nick would go to the shoe store, buy the shoes, and then head to the post office to fulfill his order. It didn't take long for him to realize that people were very comfortable ordering shoes online. The result was Zappos, the largest retailer of shoes in the world. How might we think about a minimum viable spiritual growth plan?[13]

In 2014 Leadership Network surveyed over 1,600 ministry leaders of churches with over a thousand members. They discovered that the most frequently cited issue facing churches was "discipleship." In response to a question asking where they felt their church was most innovative, the bottom two categories were "evangelistic emphasis" and "personal worship and devotional life." The area in which leaders felt weakest was "evangelistic effectiveness and spiritual growth." Devotional life, evangelism, and spiritual growth. How is it possible that the very things churches are created for and designed to do are the areas of the most perceived weakness? How could we change that? How might we transform the weakest links into the strongest links?

If you think about it, most Christian content is created by "power users" for other power users. If you are reading this book, you are probably a power user. Pastors and writers are power users. They must study and think deeply to have something worthy to share from the pen or pulpit. This discipline leads to insight and often a feeling of connection to God. So, this discipline becomes the de facto recommended prescription and path for congregants and readers. But what if people did not need huge amounts of content to be growing, effective Christ-followers? What if the church's job is not to train big-league pitchers but simply to help parents play catch with their kids in the back yard?

A few years ago, I (Eric) became acquainted with the work of BJ Fogg. Fogg is a behavior scientist at Stanford and the author of *Tiny Habits: The Small Changes That Change Everything*—his best-selling book on behavior change. Fogg says the key to behavior change comes through "tiny habits"—behaviors that are so simple to do that they are most likely to be done. In his TEDx Talk "Forget big change, start with a tiny habit," Fogg tells us that "simplicity changes behavior more than motivation" and "simplicity is easier than motivation."[14] So rather than trying to motivate people to do difficult things (like "read through the entire Bible this year" or "pray daily for five people you want to come to Christ," and so forth), help them create a plan consisting of baby steps. As people gain efficacy through consistently completing small actions, they create the desire and ability to take on more difficult actions.

## Believe, Belong, Bless

For the past few years, when I (Eric) have been meeting with church leaders, I've talked about a rhythm of growth found in the Celtic knot. The early Celtic Christians used this symbol to visualize the Trinity. The knot has no beginning and no end. Each member of the Trinity is distinct and yet an integral part of the others. The Father flows into the Son; the Son flows into the Spirit; the Spirit into the Father. To capture this same holistic rhythm, we can insert the words "Believe," "Belong," and "Bless."[15] Let's take a look at each.

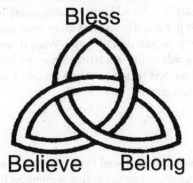

Figure 3.2

### Believe

Believing is our connection with God. A few years ago, I was in New York City and found myself sitting next to a Jewish man in a tightly packed restaurant. I asked him about his faith.

"Why do you wear the yarmulke?"

"It's a symbol of submission under God."

"Tell me about the tassels."

"The knots represent the 613 commands in the Torah."

"Do you have them memorized?"

"Every one of them."

"What do you pray?"

"A good Jew prays the same prayer every day," he replied. He recited that prayer in Hebrew and then gave me the translation: "'Lord, you have made me for a purpose. Help me walk in that purpose today.' I pray that prayer every day before I get out of bed." It hit me how such a small group of people has had such an inordinate amount of positive influence on the world, waking up every day with a sense of calling and purpose.

Maybe prayer doesn't have to be long to be effective. The Lord's Prayer can be prayed thoughtfully in around thirty seconds. What if every day we prayed a minimum viable prayer embracing and yielding all of our life to Jesus? Something like, "God, you made me for a purpose. Help me walk in that purpose with everyone I meet, everything I do, every place I go, and everything I say. Amen." It's not that we couldn't pray at other times, but a prayer like this would be the foundation of our connection with God every day.

## Belong

Belonging means connecting with and purposefully encouraging another believer every day. Hebrews 3:13 nudges us toward connection: "Encourage one another *daily*, . . . so that none of you may be hardened by sin's deceitfulness." We need encouragement *every day*. My friend Mark Howell, a small-groups guru, says, "An unconnected believer is just one life incident away from leaving the church." Without daily encouragement people do fall away. What if we did not let a day pass when we didn't speak words of life to a fellow believer? What if we would not give sleep to our eyes until we had texted or called another Christian just to express a word of hope and encouragement?

## Bless

Everyone you meet has an inherent need to be "blessed"—to be told that what they do matters—that *they* matter. A famous saying reminds us that "everyone you meet is fighting a battle; be kind." To bless means to ask God to care for and protect someone. Blessing someone is speaking words of life and hope over them. It is catching people doing something right and calling attention to it. It is stopping to breathe a few words of encouragement into the life of a young mom patiently talking to her two-year-old in the grocery store. It is pausing to tell a smiling parking attendant that he made your day. It is bringing coffee and a scone to a coworker who is struggling. Jesus talked about the importance of little acts of kindness: "If anyone gives even a cup of cold water . . ." (Matt 10:42). It's a rhythm of helping people *believe* (initially and continually in Christ), *belong* (experience life-connection with other believers in the family), and *bless* those who do not yet know Christ (for example, Gen 12:3; Ps 67:7). We believe that growing people of faith are intentionally engaged in all three practices at some level and with some consistency.

## Plus One

Whether we're talking about tiny habits or consistent practice of habits (small and large), "everything counts." That's what I (Rick) said to our LifeBridge Church family a couple years ago during a sermon series on loving our neighbors. "If you take your neighbor's trash cans in or attend a neighbor's barbecue or encourage a young mom in a grocery store—it all counts in moving a person on their journey toward Christ." I explained this as the concept of "Plus One."

Imagine a horizontal line numbered 1 to 100, from left to right. The number 1 represents a person who is about as far from God as a person can be and 100 represents that same person making a commitment to follow Christ. So any act of encouragement, thoughtfulness, servanthood, or kindness—big or small—counts in moving a person "plus one" toward Jesus.

I went on to ask the LifeBridge congregants to simply keep track of small acts of kindness or encouragement that would move people along from 1 to 2 or from 88 to 89. At the end of the week our church family had recorded, via text messaging, over 34,000 Plus Ones.

What difference would it make in your city if every person in your church had the practice of connecting with God every day, encouraging a fellow believer every day, and blessing a person outside the faith every day—something as simple as Plus One? Say you had a thousand people in your congregation. That is 365,000 Plus One connections to God every year: 365,000 words and acts of encouragement bestowed on fellow believers around the city. What's more, we are recipients as well as givers of these powerful words and acts. Each year your church has 365,000 thoughtful, positive, loving interactions with nonbelievers. We suspect that what may currently be the biggest areas of weakness in your church (evangelism, spiritual growth, and devotional life) may become your strongest areas.

If what you are currently doing is working, then by all means stick with it. But if you feel, like most churches, that you are stuck, try experimenting with the rhythms of believing, belonging, and blessing.

## Mission Statements: Turning "So What?" into "So That"

Mission drives every organization. Mission is your reason for being, the reason of your very existence as a church. A church's mission statement says a lot about whether a church exists for itself or for a purpose outside itself. Is the church a place for bodybuilding or weight training? Let's take a look at some typical church mission statements:

- To help people become fully devoted followers of Christ
- To connect people to one another and to Jesus
- To lead people into a growing relationship with Christ
- Helping people find their way back to God
- To help people take their next steps with Jesus
- To make the name of Jesus famous in our generation

All of these are good, solid, and typical of most churches' mission statements, but each one begs the question "So what?" What would be different in the world because that local church fulfilled its mission? What evil would die in the community? What good would thrive in the city? Just as weight training includes a "so that" statement ("so that I can win the state wrestling championship at 152 pounds"), so too do churches need a "so that" statement. "So that" is about impact, and impact is more about your vision of a changed community or a changed world. After all, the church doesn't exist for itself but for the world. How would your community be different if a critical mass of people

- were fully devoted followers of Christ?
- were connected to one another and to Jesus?
- had a growing relationship with Christ?
- had found their way back to God?
- took their next steps with Jesus?
- made the name of Jesus more famous?

Would there be more third-graders reading at third-grade level? Would more kids be adopted out of foster care? Would more good jobs be created? Would fewer babies be born out of wedlock? Would the divorce rate go down? Would more children have breakfast before school and food to eat on the weekends? Would infant mortality be reduced? Would the percentage of high school graduates increase? Would more kids have a mentor? Would more people know their neighbors' names? Would refugees be met and welcomed? Would upward mobility increase in your city? Would there be more open doors and open hearts to those not like us? Would more people be on mission and involved in redeeming something that is broken in our world and in living out their Ephesians 2:10 calling? If nothing is different in the world because of the changed lives in the church, what difference is the church really making?

Here's the good news: two little words, "so that," added to your mission statement can change everything.

- To help people become fully devoted followers of Christ *so that* every person in our city can experience life as God intended it.

- To connect people to one another and to Jesus *so that* together we can change the world through the power of God.

- To lead people into a growing relationship with Christ *so that* together we can be the hands, feet, and voice of Jesus in our city.

- Helping people find their way back to God *so that* they can help others find their way back to God and together we can create a thriving city.

- To help people take their next steps with Jesus *so that* together we can more fully live out the redemptive plan God has for each one of us.

- To make the name of Jesus famous in our generation *so that* people want to know him and join him in helping redeem everything that is broken in our world.

Get the idea? Another way to test the efficacy of your mission statement would be simply to add the phrase "To change the world by" at the beginning of your mission statement. You now have your de facto theory of change that you can test out.

- *To change the world by* helping people become fully devoted followers of Christ.

- *To change the world by* connecting people to one another and to Jesus.

- *To change the world by* leading people into a growing relationship with Christ.

- *To change the world by* helping people find their way back to God.

- *To change the world by* helping people take their next steps with Jesus.

- *To change the world by* making the name of Jesus famous in our generation.

The church was never intended to be a bodybuilding poser, showing off its pomp and power, blustering about its moral superiority in a broken world. Nor is the church in a bodybuilding competition with other churches in the community to see who can build the largest and most beautiful church. Christ's church, from the beginning, has always been the training center staffed with apostles, prophets, evangelists, pastors, and teachers whose sole function is to equip God's people for works of service. If done right, church is a place where God's athletes, after stacking hands, find themselves saying, "Let's go fix something!" or "Let's go build something!" That's what weight-training churches are about.

## The Leadership Challenge

Lately, when I (Eric) have the opportunity to address a church audience, I'll ask this question: "How many here want to change the world? If you want to change the world, raise your hand." With the exception of those who are writing down the question, every hand goes up.

And then while the hands are still raised, I often add this caveat: "Isn't it sad how few people are regularly given the opportunity to do so? What if this church became the place where people could regularly be given the opportunity to engage the world in such a way that it would somehow be different, that something or someone would be better because of them? At the end of the year, what if your one evaluative question to every person under your watch was expressed in the question 'How has God used you to change the world this past year?'"

Could you imagine what it would be like to have a congregation of fifty, five hundred, or five thousand, each with an answer to that question and a story to tell? The job of a leader is to provide the theology, motivation, and opportunity for every Christ-follower to have a positive answer to that question. If everyone wants to change the world, then why not structure church so that people are given regular opportunities to do so?

# 4.

## Story: They Live in the Kingdom Story, Not a Church Story

*When our works supersede our words, God's kingdom shows up.*

—Murray Robertson, senior pastor, Spreydon Baptist Church, Christchurch, New Zealand

A few years ago, I (Eric) and a good buddy of mine attended a three-day seminar called "Story" led by the screenwriter Robert McKee. McKee's former students, including Peter Jackson, Russell Brand, Jimmy Fallon, Julia Roberts, Kirk Douglas, David Bowie, Meg Ryan, and many more, have garnered sixty-five Academy Awards and two hundred Emmy Awards for their screenwriting.

Many of the movies and TV shows you enjoy, such as *Forrest Gump, The Da Vinci Code, CSI*, and *Law and Order*, are products of McKee's students. Donald Miller (author of *Blue Like Jazz*) got the idea of launching his Story Brand business after attending McKee's Story seminar.

The seminar was an incredible experience and one I continually recommend. McKee began by telling us that the world has an insatiable appetite for stories. We just can't get enough of them. He said, "Writing a great story is why God put you on this earth." McKee, who was in his late sixties at the time, lectured from 9:00 a.m. until 8:30 p.m. for three consecutive days, allowing only three fifteen-minute breaks and one hour for lunch. There was no interaction, just straight lecture—and all eighty people in attendance loved every moment. All of us were amazed at his skill and coveted his passion for communication. He is a student of humanity. The things he said about story-writing were very insightful. "A great story does two things: first, it transports you to a world you've never been to, and second, once you are there, you find yourself in the story." Wow! Think about your favorite movies or stories. Isn't that what they do?

Jesus was this kind of storyteller. The story of the good Samaritan transports us to a place we've never been to (on the road leading from Jerusalem to Jericho), and once we are there, we find ourselves in the story—as priest, Levite, bystander, victim, Samaritan, innkeeper, or donkey. In the parable of the prodigal son, where are we? Who are we? McKee, quoting Aristotle, says that the ending of a story should give listeners what they want—but not what they expect. This is probably why parables are so memorable. They give us surprise endings. It is the unlikely Samaritan who is the hero. It is the father putting his best robe on the shoulders of his rebellious son. It is all the laborers receiving the same wage even though they worked for differing lengths of time.

## What Kind of Story Have We Been Telling?

Tim Keller, pastor of Redeemer Presbyterian Church, New York City, New York, tells us that "every 'worldview' has to answer the question: 'what is wrong with life and how can it be fixed?' Every worldview singles out some part of the good creation as being the main source of the problem (thus 'demonizing' something) and singles out some other part of the fallen creation as being the main solution."[1] So a Marxist worldview would have one diagnosis and one cure, as would a moralist, a free-market economist, a right-wing conservative, a left-wing liberal, and an evangelical Christian. The story or worldview most Christians have adopted, believed, and shared with others, using Keller's construct, goes something like this: "What is wrong with the world is sin—humanity's rebellion against God. People were created to have a relationship with God, but they sinned against God and that relationship with God was broken. What was the solution? Jesus came to earth, lived a sinless life, and so was able to die in our place. Jesus's death and resurrection make it possible for people who put their faith in him to be restored to a relationship with God and go to heaven when they die. As more people are transformed through a right relationship with God, societies are transformed and our world is changed."

This is all true—but it's not complete. It is personal but not comprehensive. The facts are correct, but that's not the story. In the paraphrased words of the English novelist E. M. Forster, "A fact is that the queen died and the king died. A story is that the queen died and the king died of a broken heart."[2] Is there a fuller story for us to tell?

## The Rest of the Story

A fuller or thicker story for us to share might go something like this:

In the beginning, when God created the world, everything was good. Man and woman's relationship with God was good; both man and woman had a healthy, robust view of themselves (after all, they were fashioned by God). Adam and Eve had a whole and beneficial relationship with each other, and the only way to describe their relationship with the world they lived in was "good." In Eden there was wholeness. Man and woman lived in harmony with their environment and talked freely and openly with God and with each other. They were knowing recipients of God's good gifts. There was physical work to be done in the garden, tending plants and nurturing fruit-bearing trees. They were told they could eat and enjoy the fruits of their labor. There was other work to be done as well—work that summoned the best of their creativity in naming the animals, with the finality that "whatever the man called each living creature, that was its name" (Gen 2:19).

Man and woman were not only in *fellowship* with God; they were in *partnership* with God—perhaps not full partners, but junior partners. God created the living plants in the garden, but the man was given the responsibility to "work [the garden] and take care of it" (Gen 2:15). God created all the animals and birds (Gen 2:19), but entrusted to the man the responsibility of naming each one. The climate was such that the man and the woman had no need of clothing and there was seemingly no need, or at least no mention, of permanent shelter.

In this idyllic setting, God was clearly in charge. It was his domain, and he set boundaries defining what was and was not permissible. Man lived in harmony with woman—a partner taken from his own flesh. Her well-being was attached to and could not be separated from his well-being and his good. Together man and woman were stewards and trustees of the earth.

But then, as in all good stories, something happened—the inciting incident.

## The Inciting Incident

The Fall is what McKee would call the "inciting incident." The inciting incident is the scene in the story that throws life out of balance and begs for resolution. This great story's inciting incident was called "sin," and everything changed. Man's relationship with God was broken. I imagine that when Adam and Eve were walking out of Eden after being expelled, Adam may have turned to Eve and said something like, "OK, we really blew it, and I do feel a bit of spiritual emptiness, but this is still a great place to live." But sin's reach affected their sense of self (shame and guilt that resulted in hiding from God) and their personal relationships. Imagine the pain and grief when Adam and Eve discovered that one of their boys was dead and the other was a murderer! Adam probably turned to Eve and most likely uttered the first curse word, something like "#@&*! This sin thing is way bigger than I imagined."

Sin affected humanity's relationship not only with God, self, and one another but also with the environment—the world God had placed them in. No longer would the earth bring forth its fruit as it had. Adam and Eve would have to labor to make the earth productive. Moreover, the earth was now broken, and there would be earthquakes, tornados, hurricanes, erupting volcanoes, and tsunamis that would ripple down through millennia, randomly destroying both property and innocent lives (Luke 13:4). Romans 8:22 reminds us that because of sin, the "whole creation has been groaning as in the pains of childbirth right up to the present time."

Brokenness was not the way that God intended things to be. It was the aberration of a broken world filled with violence or indifference toward and hatred of neighbor, exploitation of the weak, tribal factions, pride, covetousness, drunkenness, marital strife, conniving, and chicanery.

Once the people in the audience hearing and watching the story see the inciting incident, they know a scene is coming that will resolve the conflict and restore a new balance. There must be another scene—the "mandatory scene."

# The "Mandatory Scene"

This "mandatory scene," as McKee calls it, is necessary for all stories. Our mandatory scene is the redemptive plan that God would bring forth through Jesus. In the fullness of time, God's Son came to earth and lived his life doing exactly what God the Father wanted him to do, culminating with his death on the cross to pay for the sin of the whole world. Jesus didn't die only to restore humanity's relationship with God (as if that were not enough); his death is the basis of making people whole, bringing reconciliation between people and with creation. The apostle Paul tells us in Colossians 1:19–20, "For God was pleased to have all his fullness dwell in [Christ], and through him to reconcile to himself all things, whether things on earth or things in heaven, by making peace through his blood, shed on the cross."

Everything that was lost in the Fall was redeemed through the cross and will one day be fully restored (Rev 21:1). After Jesus's conversation and interaction with Zacchaeus, he says, "For the Son of Man came to seek and to save *that which was lost*" (Luke 19:10). Certainly, he came to seek and save *the lost,* but even more important, he came to seek and save *what* was lost. Everything that sin and the Fall took away, Jesus came to restore and make new. That's what makes the gospel such incredibly good news!

In response to the observable brokenness of the world, we often hear people today say, "It is what it is." But we believe there is more. As Christ-followers, we should find ourselves saying, "It is what it is, but it's not as God intends it to be, as it can be, and as it someday will be."

# An Unexpected Ending

McKee said that the ending of a story should give hearers what they want but not what they expect. The Austrian philosopher and priest Ivan Illich "was once asked what is the most revolutionary way to change society. Is it violent revolution or is it gradual reform? He gave a careful answer. Neither. If you want to change society, then you must tell an alternative story."[3] Where's the unexpected in our stories? We've been telling the church story and are currently living out the consequences of that story. But what if we understood and told the kingdom story?

## The Role of Conflict

McKee informs us that there is no story without conflict. "These men who have caused trouble all over the world have now come here. . . . They are all defying Caesar's decrees, saying that there is another king, one called Jesus" (Acts 17:6–7). The kingship of Jesus was an affront to the kingdom of Caesar, and that was enough conflict to warrant the death of Jesus and persecution of the disciples. McKee also tells us that there is no love story without a rival. The love story of the gospel is between Jesus and his Bride (the church), and Satan is rivaling for our affection and allegiance. This creates what is recognized as a love triangle.

### Choice Defines Character

Every scene in the movie ends with a choice that defines the character of the central actors. The harder the choice, the better defined the character becomes. Now imagine the ending to this scene filled with conflict and choice. Jesus is in the garden praying fervently, "Father, all things are possible with you, and if it is possible, take this cup from me . . . yet not as I will, but as you will." And Jesus makes the toughest, most character-defining choice he could make. He will go to the cross and rise from the dead on our behalf. It's not the ending anyone expected, but it is the ending all of humanity needs and is grateful for.

## The Importance of the Kingdom

When we explore the stories Jesus told, we often find that "the kingdom of God" plays a central role. But how important is this kingdom? The word *kingdom* is mentioned 152 times in the New Testament and 116 times in the Gospels (NIV). (By contrast, the word *church* is mentioned just three times in the Gospels—all in the book of Matthew.) The first public words of John the Baptist and Jesus in the Gospel of Matthew were to announce the kingdom (Matt 3:2; 4:17). One of the requests in the prayer Jesus taught his disciples was "Your kingdom come . . ." (Matt 6:10). Jesus taught that the first priority of the believer is to seek God's kingdom (Matt 6:33). The kingdom was to be the central message of the apostles' teaching (Matt 10:7), and the "bookend" passages of Acts (1:3; 28:31) are about the proclamation of the kingdom. The apostle Paul mentioned the kingdom no fewer than sixteen times in his writing and speeches. So how did we lose our focus on the kingdom? Why has the kingdom been relegated to a future residence? How was "kingdom" co-opted and replaced by "church"?

In his book *The Unshakable Kingdom and the Unchanging Person*, the great missionary statesman E. Stanley Jones writes:

> The three historic creeds, summing up Christian thought and doctrine among them, mention once what Jesus mentioned a hundred times. The greatest loss that has ever come to the Christian movement in its long course in history was this loss of the Kingdom. For the thing that Jesus called the Good News, the Gospel, has been lost. Not silenced, but lost as the directive of the movement. The Christian movement went riding off in all directions without goal and without power to move on to that goal. The substitutes became the goal. A crippled Christianity went across the Western world, leaving a crippled result. A vacuum was created in the soul of Christendom; the Kingdom of God became an individual experience now and a collective experience in heaven. Vast areas of life were left out, unredeemed—the economic, the social, and the political.[4]

All this talk of the kingdom begs the question "What is the kingdom?" The answer we've come up with is that "the kingdom of God is any place over which God has operative dominion." Although God is the creator of everything and everyone (Ps 24:1), the kingdom of God extends to those social structures, geographical areas, or regions of the human heart where God's rule is effective. The kingdom is where the king is reigning. So, if Jesus is reigning as king in your own life, "the kingdom of God is in your midst" (Luke 17:21). If you are searching for a simpler definition of the kingdom, try this one, offered by Reggie McNeal: The kingdom is simply "life as God intended it."

The kingdom is often referred to as being both "present and not yet," meaning that the reign of God is currently active but will one day culminate in the full expression of God's reign. That will be the day when "the kingdom of the world has become the kingdom of our Lord and of his Messiah, and he will reign for ever and ever" (Rev 11:15). That's a great ending!

## Comparing the Church and the Kingdom

What happened to the kingdom? Perhaps it is helpful to distinguish between kingdom and church. In doing so, we admire the words of Howard Snyder: "Kingdom people seek first the kingdom of God and its justice; church people often put church work above concerns of justice, mercy and truth. Church people think about how to get people into the church; Kingdom people think about how to get the church into the world. Church people worry that the world might change the church; Kingdom people work to see the church change the world."[5] We sometimes forget that God designed the church to be a means by which God's kingdom is realized and made visible in our communities. The church does not exist for itself. The church exists to proclaim and demonstrate that the kingdom is near.

What's the biggest difference between "church thinking" and "kingdom thinking"? Here's a comparison we've come up with; you can probably make your own additions.

| Church | Kingdom |
| --- | --- |
| Local | Global |
| Internal focus | External focus |
| Great Commission | Great Commandment as basis for Great Commission |
| Propositional truth | God's narrative story |
| Monologue | Dialogue |
| Exclusive | Inclusive |
| At center of society | Central to society |

| | |
|---|---|
| Evangelism is the goal | Evangelism is starting point |
| Stairstep growth | Journey |
| Programs | Relational |
| Gospel of salvation | Gospel of the kingdom |
| Proclamation evangelism | Proclamation and demonstration |
| The gospel explained | The gospel lived out |
| Sunday | Every day |
| Addresses only the soul | Affects all aspects of society |
| Rapture—escape mentality | Material, social, earthly, secular |
| Sacred vs. secular | Integration of sacred in the secular |
| Growing *my* church | Growing *the* church |
| Focus on transaction | Focus on transformation |
| You go to church | Wherever the church is, you encounter the kingdom |

## What Is Kingdom Work?

In the broadest sense, anytime we are involved in making this world more reflective of what God will ultimately make of it in the coming kingdom, we are involved in kingdom work. A bigger, thicker story creates a space for those who are not yet members of God's kingdom to be engaged in kingdom work through medicine, teaching, peacemaking, adoption of orphans, drought relief, HIV/AIDS ministry, anti-trafficking, providing clean drinking water, and other causes.

Here's something to think about: Millions of people around the world are aware of the fact that "things aren't the way they are supposed to be"—that something is broken. N. T. Wright, in his book *Simply Christian*, refers to this awareness as echoes of the voice of God that remind every person that something is fractured and flawed, that things are not the way God created them to be. The four echoes are

- the longing for justice,
- the quest for spirituality,
- the hunger for relationships, and
- the delight in beauty.[6]

Those compassionate souls who are working to end sex trafficking or to dig wells in Africa are listening to the echoes and recognize that they are fixing something that is broken. Those who are concerned about global climate change, water pollution, and the number of carbon dioxide particles circulating in the air may be passionate about fixing those things because they sense that things aren't what they are supposed to be. They may not know the theology, but they do know that all of creation is groaning as it awaits redemption, and they want to be part of that redemption. Rather than writing this very large segment of society off as secularists, liberals, environmentalists, or the like, why not use this common awareness of brokenness to connect them to the larger story? What if, anytime we met a person who exhibited one or more of these echoes, we could see the echoes as on-ramps to deeper spiritual conversation? These echoes could be proxy data for God stirring in a person's life. That's a great conversation to enter into!

Daniel Pink, in *A Whole New Mind*, writes, "Humans are not ideally set up to understand logic; they are ideally set up to understand stories."[7] More important, we believe they long to be part of a meaningful story. After all, there are no bit players in the story God is writing. Some people sense that people are disconnected from God; others sense a certain solidarity with those who hurt; still others sense the brokenness of the world. Some want to save lives, others want to save the planet, and others want to save souls. The point is that all of these can play a part in God's redemptive story.

## Isn't This Work for the Church to Do?

Yes! And God would love to use the church first, but when the church isn't paying attention, God will raise up others who will do the work. God raised up Artaxerxes (Ezra 4), Cyrus (a figure throughout Ezra and in other passages), and Nebuchadnezzar (appearing in 2 Kings, 2 Chron, Ezra, and elsewhere), whom he describes as his tools to accomplish his work. With this in mind, we see that there is plenty of room for the likes of Bill and Melinda Gates, Warren Buffett, Bono, Richard Branson, and Mark and Priscilla Chan Zuckerberg to carry out God's bigger story. God's kingdom work is accomplished by believers and nonbelievers—often working side by side.

Who fetched the water for Jesus's first miracle in John 2? Not the believing disciples; it was the servants who fetched the water and brought the wine to the wine steward. It was the "Asiarchs," the secular officials of Ephesus, who were identified as "friends" of Paul who gave him good counsel (Acts 19:30–32 NASB). The best advice and counsel Moses received was from his father-in-law, Jethro, a Midianite priest (Exod 18; Deut 1). God's work often involves people of good faith working alongside people of goodwill to fix things they commonly care about. We'll talk more of these unlikely partnerships in chapter 6.

## Becoming Part of the Kingdom

At this point, it is important to clarify that kingdom work does not in any way accomplish one's entrance into God's kingdom (Matt 7:21–23). Jesus gave the crystal-clear requisite for entering the kingdom of heaven in John 3. In his discourse with Nicodemus, Jesus told him, "Very truly I tell you, no one can see the kingdom of God unless they are born again. . . . Very truly I tell you, no one can enter the kingdom of God unless they are born of water and the Spirit" (John 3:3–5). Anyone and everyone who enters the kingdom will come through the same door as Nicodemus—by faith.

## Great Commandment, Great Commission, and Great Compassion

Three "Great" passages are found in the book of Matthew: the *Great Commandment*—"Love God with all your heart, soul, mind, and strength, and love your neighbor as yourself"; the *Great Commission*—"Make disciples of all the nations"; and the passage less commonly known as one of these "Greats," the *Great Compassion* in Matthew 25—"As you did it to the least of these, you did it to me." We tell a better story by modeling a better story and inviting others to be a part of that story. The acts of mercy depicted in Matthew 25:31–46 (feeding the hungry, giving water to the thirsty, welcoming the stranger, clothing the naked, comforting the sick, and visiting the prisoner) would be a good starting point for any church or individual that desires to be more kingdom-minded. These are not church-growth strategies but rather an extension of what Jesus wants his church to be doing in the world and something for which we will need to give an account. We do these acts of mercy not to convert others but because we ourselves have been converted. Are you doing anything to feed, provide clean water, clothe, welcome, comfort, or visit those who need to experience God's touch on their lives?

A very popular question in recent years has been "What would Jesus do?" It's a good question, but to determine what Jesus would do, we must look at what he did. In the Gospels, we see Jesus looking at the community (people) with compassion. We see him disrupting the tired, worn-out ways in which things had always been done. We see him meeting physical needs while also engaging spiritual needs. Jesus clearly viewed the world through kingdom lenses.

## If Jesus Were Mayor

Back in 2004, Bob Moffitt of Harvest Foundation released a book titled *If Jesus Were Mayor*. What a fascinating thought as it relates to the kingdom of God! How would things be different if Jesus were in charge? What kind of story would unfold? Moffitt poses these profound questions:

- What would He do about street children and the homeless?
- What would He do about alcoholism, drug abuse, and other addictions?
- How would He strengthen families?
- How would He promote safe drinking water, adequate housing and food, health services, garbage and sewer systems, and decent roads?
- What would He do about fair wages and adequate employment?
- What would He do about unwanted children and care for the sick and elderly?
- What would He do to bring beauty—clean streets, trees, flowers, and public parks?
- What would He do in the education of children and adults?[8]

This is a challenging thought, isn't it? But when we are praying, "Thy kingdom come, thy will be done on earth as it is in heaven," isn't this what we are asking for, the practical expression of Jesus's reign? What would it look like to pray, "Thy kingdom come, thy will be done in [your city] as it is in heaven"? What would your city look like if the kingdom of God really took shape there?

## Vintage Vineyard

What happens when a church engages outside its walls? Could a kingdom-minded, externally focused church really help bring about some of the transformation that Bob Moffitt posits is possible? In 2007, Reggie McNeal and I (Eric), through Leadership Network, started something called the Missional Renaissance Leadership Community. This community met four times for two days each time over an eighteen-month period, and was made up of ten senior pastors, who were each asked to bring along an associate pastor, a city official, a CEO of a business, or an executive director of a major nonprofit organization. This first community was great! We had mayors, executive directors of United Way and a major art museum, the CEOs of nationally known businesses, and an array of talented, passionate leaders. By gathering together with cross-domain leaders, Reggie and I hoped to accomplish things church leaders alone could not accomplish—and we were not disappointed. Because Leadership Network is adamant about measurement, they got back some very positive results before the third gathering. Summing up the accomplishments of the previous six months, Executive Pastor Will Shearer from Vineyard Church in Columbus, Ohio, reported on some of the progress that was made:

- Recruited over two hundred new volunteers to serve in community justice–oriented ministries—prison ministry, free health clinic, free legal clinic, after-school programs, and the like.

- Held a three-day "justice revival" with more than forty churches and denominations; total attendance for the three evenings exceeded ten thousand people called to action in response to Jesus and his concern for the poor and marginalized in the community. Each night, an invitation to receive Christ was issued, with hundreds of people responding.

- Legislative initiatives: Dan Franz, Vineyard's pastor for urban and mercy ministries, had been taking a lead role among central Ohio pastors speaking out in the "public square" about the payday lending and gambling industries. Legislation limiting the rate of interest charged by the payday lending industry (reducing the APR from 391 percent to 28 percent) was passed by the Ohio General Assembly.

- Vineyard Columbus sent out forty-one teams to pass out grocery bags, clean up houses and yards, and do a variety of similar service projects.

- Mentor training: Vineyard partnered with Columbus public schools and Big Brothers Big Sisters of Central Ohio to recruit and train more than fifty new mentors (most of them from Vineyard) to serve one hour per week in Columbus schools as one-on-one mentors with middle school and high school students. This is part of Project Mentor (sponsored by Nationwide Insurance to the tune of $600,000), the goal of which was to line up ten thousand mentors by 2012 to serve in Columbus public schools.

- In collaboration with the office of the mayor, Vineyard held a "dropout prevention summit" in October 2009.

- In collaboration with the nonprofit sector, Vineyard Community Center's free legal clinic has initiated with the other prominent free legal clinics in Columbus the hosting of a series of "debtors' rights" workshops to help individuals facing home foreclosure or personal bankruptcy.

- In collaboration with the private sector, Vineyard Community Center has developed a volunteer-led career development program (including career coaches and job search workshops) and is now partnering with a privately owned human resource firm to launch job training and job placement activities as well. The center has also partnered with local banks to host personal finance workshops focusing on budgeting, credit card debt, and the like.

Furthermore, Lead Pastor Rich Nathan drafted a working document titled "Toward the Common Good," which he presented to state legislators as an outline for social reform that included promotion of marriage, welfare reform, divorce reform, adoption reform, livable-wage legislation, the importance of fatherhood, helping children of prisoners, and the reintegration of prisoners into society. This document has helped define how the faith community and government can work together to solve problems people care about.

## A Story That Changes the World

What is the story we've been telling? Often our story presents the gospel as a rescuing force as opposed to an empowering force in our lives. The gospel is a call to safety and refuge rather than a call to adventure. Jesus did nothing less than call people to follow him in his kingdom ventures. And he's still doing the same thing today. Pastor Bob Roberts says:

> I once believed that if I could just get a person "saved" and coming to church, that would change the world. I was wrong. The gospel of the kingdom and the gospel of salvation both get conversions. The difference is that the gospel of salvation is finished at conversion. The gospel of the kingdom begins at conversion and engages comprehensively and holistically the entire person and community. It takes Matthew 25 seriously. You aren't fighting culture; you're creating a new culture by letting the gospel engage every domain of humanity, health, education, economics, communication, art, agriculture, and so on.[9]

Externally focused ministry focuses on the kingdom rather than the church in that there are many things externally focused churches engage in that do not directly benefit the church itself. People may come to faith in Christ and join another fellowship. Kids at the elementary school may all learn how to read, but the fruit of a commitment to a local school may not be realized for twenty years. If churches only have a local church perspective, eventually the business manager or executive pastor will say something like "We've been doing this externally focused ministry for a couple years now; what has been the result in our attendance and giving?" If the direction has not been "up and to the right," most likely the conclusion will be "Let's try something else." We'd like to be able to report that all externally focused, kingdom-minded churches grow dramatically, and some pastors do swear by the growth they have seen, but the truth is that some churches grow and some don't.

## A Glimpse of the Kingdom in Huntsville, Texas

What we can say is that many of the things you do will bear fruit in people's lives, in other churches, or in the community. A few years ago, I (Eric) was in Dallas speaking at a conference on becoming an externally focused church. During one of the first breaks in the session, a man introduced himself as David Valentine, pastor of the First Baptist Church in Huntsville, Texas. He introduced his church by saying it "ran around five hundred in church and three hundred in Sunday school every week." Then he told the most amazing story:

> One thing you may not know is that Huntsville Prison is the release point for prisoners in the criminal justice system in the state of Texas. Five days a week, up to 150 prisoners are released into society. They are given the clothes on their back, $75, and a one-way bus ticket. Not surprisingly, most of them find their way back to prison within a year or two. About five years ago, we began sending around a hundred of our folks

over to the prison to begin working with soon-to-be-released prisoners—helping them with jobs, clothing, connecting with family, and the like. It made such a difference in the lives of these prisoners that the prison officials asked us if we knew of any other churches in Texas that might have a similar interest in working with prisoners. So, we started working on that. Last year, of the seventy-five thousand prisoners who were released back into the state of Texas, we were able to connect forty thousand of them with caring believers and churches in the communities they were returning to.

David, his staff, and his church have a kingdom mindset. When I asked him if his church had grown much in the last five years, he responded that the church membership was around five hundred then, and five hundred now. But if you are a pastor, what would you rather have, a church of five hundred and a kingdom impact on forty thousand or a church of forty thousand and an impact on five hundred? Every week, David's church members also send volunteer teams to minister to nearly twelve hundred correctional officers and Texas Department of Criminal Justice staff, bringing snacks, soft drinks, bottled water, and an occasional lunch. When asked why they are doing this, they answer, "Because we love people and want to make a difference in their lives." They are on call to minister to staff and families of prisoners as the need arises. Their love and service have not gone unnoticed. Over the years they have received various awards from both inside their denominational family and from the larger community.

We imagine that when David goes to bed at night, he falls asleep quickly. We imagine that when he wakes up, he has a bounce in his step because he has ceased trying to create the best church *in* the community but may very well have created the best church *for* the community.

## The Leadership Challenge

Robert McKee says the test of a good movie is that you walk out saying to yourself, "That was a great story." As a leader, what story are you telling? What story are you inviting people into? McKee says a good movie has you asking throughout it, "What happens next?" as opposed to "Where is this thing going?" People who are sitting in church are asking the same types of questions. They are either asking, "Where is this thing going?" or "What happens next?" As leaders, we need to create a compelling story that every person longs to be a part of.

# 5.

# Missions: The Few Sending the Many, Not the Many Sending the Few

*In crossing cultures, the missionary teacher becomes a learner, the one who is in possession of divine revelation discovers new truth, and he who seeks the salvation of others finds himself converted all over again.*

—David Smith, *Mission after Christendom*[1]

When I (Eric) first began identifying and convening externally focused churches in 2003, church leaders were adamant about distinguishing between local and global ministry—between community ministry and "foreign missions." It just made sense. Externally focused ministry was limited to a congregation's community engagement. Four years later, as I was convening my fifth externally focused leadership community with Leadership Network, I began getting pushback from the participants who were not separating local ministry from global ministry. In our flattened world, they wanted to take what they were learning overseas and bring it back home and take what they were learning at home and bring it overseas. Many ministry leaders had assumed the leadership over all local and global ministries. Leaders like our friend Bob Roberts were increasingly using the hybrid term *glocal* to convey the thought that externally focused ministry had to include the world. I also began to get a number of requests that made me aware that something new was happening in global missions. The calls and emails went something like this: "I know you know a lot of people who are doing cool things around the world. Do you know of any good global outreach people? But don't send me any 'missions pastors' who just want to divide the missions budget pie and hold a missions fair every couple of years."

We began to sense that God was doing something new in the area of global missions because our world was changing. In times past, an effective missions program was measured by how many missionaries had been sent out from the church. "Missions" was a specialty ministry for the dedicated few who were sent and supported by the congregation. The quality and effectiveness of missions was manifested through pictures, yarn, and maps. The more yarn, the better the missions program. But as pastors rediscovered their equipping role (Eph 4:11–13) and opened their missional eyes, they discovered that everyone can play and everyone can go.

61

Most externally focused churches want to be the best church for the community *and* for the world. More and more Christ-followers are engaging locally *and* globally, and the numbers bear this out. Between 2000 and 2009, "12 percent of active churchgoers reported having gone overseas on a short-term mission project while in their teens . . . up from 5 percent in the 1990s, 4 percent in the 1980s, and only 2 percent before that."[2] More churches are engaging globally—above and beyond financial support of missionaries. Approximately one-third of US congregations send mission teams overseas, averaging eighteen members every year.[3]

However, part of the increase in global engagement may be due to what is sometimes called "missio-tourism"—where church people put their missional toe in the water, take a few pictures of poor people, and then return home, having checked off the Mission Trip box on their bucket list. As one missions leader told us, "There was a woman in church who told me, 'I've always wanted to go to France but couldn't afford to, so when I heard we were sending a team to Paris and the church would pay half the costs, it was a slam dunk for me.' That's when I knew we needed to rethink missions."

Strategies and tactics that served the church for decades are no longer working or at least not working as effectively as they have in the past. New global wine is calling for new global wineskins, and we feel that a book on the externally focused church would not be complete unless we addressed what we are seeing happening with churches that are effectively engaging not just across the street or across the tracks but across the world. We'll explain what we mean.

When Jesus left his marching orders to the early church, part of his commission included the scope of its mission. It was to make disciples in Jerusalem (the place where it was), Judaea (the country that contained Jerusalem), Samaria (the country to the north, populated by people the Jews historically despised), and to the ends of the earth. These four domains—Jerusalem, Judaea, Samaria, and the world—represent different combinations of culture and geography, as depicted in figure 5.1.

- *Across the street:* This is your Jerusalem—reaching people who are like you and who live, work, and play within geographical proximity.

- *Across the country:* This is your Judaea—reaching people who are culturally similar to you but geographically distant.

- *Across the tracks:* This is your Samaria—reaching people who are geographically close but culturally different.

- *Across the seas:* This is your "ends of the earth" ministry—reaching people who are both culturally different and geographically distant.

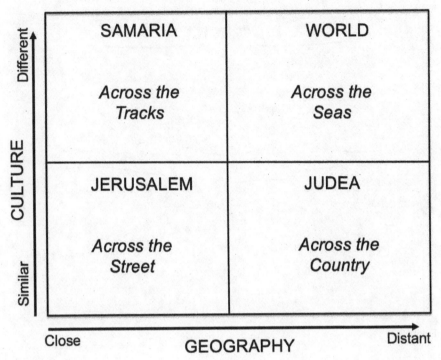

Figure 5.1

## The Changing Centers of Christianity

The big news for us in America is this: the center of Christianity has made a seismic shift from the western to the eastern hemisphere and from the northern to the southern hemisphere. That is big news. On a beautiful July afternoon, I (Eric) strolled down the Pearl Street Mall in Boulder, Colorado, and stopped in at Art Source International, one of the largest purveyors of antique maps in the world. Browsing through the "Rare Maps" section, I stumbled on a document from an 1886 atlas titled *The Distribution of Christian Religions throughout the World* that visually depicted the number of Protestant, Catholic, and Orthodox believers in various countries and regions of the world. What a gold mine! Here's what this document, more than a century old, revealed (and it's even better in color!):

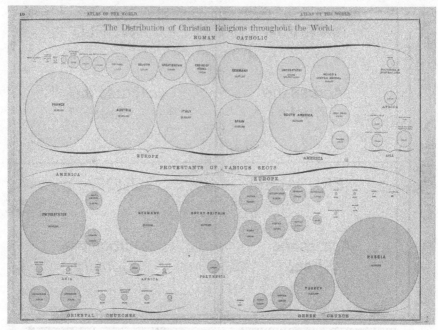

Figure 5.2

- France had the most Roman Catholics (35.5 million), followed by Austria, the nations of South America, Italy, Spain, and Germany.

- The United States, with 30 million Protestants, led Germany, Great Britain, Sweden, Russia, Austria, and the Netherlands.

- Russia was the dominant Orthodox country, maintaining the allegiance of over 54 million adherents, followed by Turkey, Austria, and Greece.

- The continent of Africa had a mere 709,000 Protestants (fewer than Polynesia) and 1.1 million Catholics.

- India had only 300,000 Protestants, and the Arabian region, Turkey, Persia (Iran), and China had a paltry 89,000 altogether.

- Christianity's center of gravity was the United States and Europe.

But interestingly, 1886 was a time when God began to wake up the church in the West to the needs of the world. A year earlier, the "Cambridge Seven" packed their bags for China. In 1886, the Student Volunteer Movement launched as one hundred university and seminary students at D. L. Moody's conference grounds at Mount Hermon, Massachusetts, signed the Princeton Pledge, which says, "I purpose, God willing, to become a foreign missionary." By the following year, those hundred students were serving in the four corners of the globe. In 1888, Jonathan Goforth sailed for China and John R. Mott was appointed chairman of the Student Volunteer Movement, whose motto was "The evangelization of the world in this generation." In 1890, Central American Mission (CAM) was founded by C. I. Scofield, for which the Scofield Reference Bible was named. In the same year, Charles Gabriel wrote the missionary song "Send the Light" and John Livingston Nevius of China launched a ministry in Korea. In 1891, Samuel Zwemer went to Arabia and Helen Chapman sailed for the Congo. And in 1895, Africa Inland Mission was formed by Peter Cameron Scott, the Japan Bible Society was established, and Amy Carmichael arrived in India. The missionaries had started their work, and their work made a global difference.

Philip Jenkins, in his book *The Next Christendom*, writes:

> Until recently, the overwhelming majority of Christians have lived in White nations, allowing theorists to speak smugly, arrogantly, of 'European Christian' civilization. Over the past century, however, the center of gravity in the Christian world has shifted inexorably southward, to Africa, Asia, and Latin America. Already today, the largest Christian communities on the planet are to be found in Africa and Latin America.[4]

Jenkins goes on to quote Kenyan scholar John Mbiti, who notes that "the centers of the church's universality [are] no longer in Geneva, Rome, Athens, Paris, London, [and] New York, but Kinshasa, Buenos Aires, Addis Ababa, and Manila."[5]

As of 2006, the largest churches in the world were not in Southern California or Texas. In fact, "none of the fifty largest churches in the world are found in North America."[6] In 2002, Jenkins wrote, "The Full Gospel Central Church in Seoul now has over half a million members, earning it a place in the *Guinness Book of World Records* as the world's largest single congregation on earth."[7] *Megachurch* does not begin to describe a church of this size. Indeed, "there are almost twice as many Presbyterians in South Korea as in the United States."[8]

## Missionaries from Other Countries

According to a 2006 article in *Christianity Today*, "South Korea sends more missionaries than any country but the U.S. And it won't be long before it's number one."[9] This is not just a dream but a plan. The Korea Mission Association plans "to send 100,000 full-time Korean missionaries by 2030.

"Currently over 3,700 Nigerians are serving as missionaries with a hundred agencies in more than fifty countries [and] now it's becoming a major missionary-sending country. For every missionary who now enters Nigeria, five Nigerians go out as missionaries to other fields of service."[10] In our own community of Boulder, Colorado, we welcomed an Anglican missionary from Africa who had come here to reach people with the gospel. In the fall of 2019 a group of pastors from Stavanger, Norway, through Agenda One (agenda1.no) began convening and leading the staff of the largest churches in Boulder as a two-year learning community. The center of gravity has shifted.

## The Big Shifts

To address the changing face of missions, God is raising up churches, and leaders of those churches, who are painting a different picture of missions. They are telling a different story. They are making the shift from top-down to mutuality, from proclamation of the gospel to both proclamation and demonstration of the gospel, from local and global missions being separate to global and local residing under one ministry department. These leaders are the new generation of missional leaders in the iteration of missions that has shifted from long-term expatriates to long-term commitments with short-term vocational teams. These entrepreneurial leaders have long-term relationships but travel in and out of countries as easily as leaders drove across town a generation ago. With the flattening of the world and the immediacy and economy of global communication, leaders are figuring new ways to influence the world. Missionaries who try to have a "business cover" are being replaced with businesspeople who are living out the gospel. Individual missionaries are being replaced with small groups of people who are living missionally. Innovative, leading churches find themselves partnering not based on denomination but with those who share a like commitment. Church leaders are no longer raising mission funds just from the congregation, but churches are raising resources from the community to help sponsor hospitals, water projects, and other ventures of common concern.

The cultural ethos of missions back in the late twentieth century went something like this: We in America have everything—the tools, strategies, technologies, and training to reach the world. We just need to mobilize our people and go. So, we went—sending people out as long-term missionaries, short-term missionaries, and sending others on *Jesus* film and vision trips, and it worked. But something in missions was shifting underfoot.

## The Present Future

William Gibson observes that "the future is already here—it's just not evenly distributed."[11] We agree. All around us are examples of innovators and early adopters who have discovered new principles—more effective ways of thinking, being, and doing that have yet to become the dominant or prevailing way of living. But it is only a matter of time.

In 2009, I (Eric) interviewed over fifty leaders of large churches that were already engaged in global outreach. Each interview lasted about an hour and covered what the leader and their church were doing globally. Each leader brought passion and insight to the conversation. Each of them was eager to explain what they were doing but also to learn from others who walked in similar global shoes.

Based on those interviews with missional leaders, along with our own experience and reading, we take the remainder of this chapter to introduce eight trends we think will shape the future of missions.

## Mutuality

The future of missions will be shaped by mutuality between East and West, North and South, and sending and receiving nations. Because there are now vibrant believers and thriving churches in Africa, Asia, Latin America, Eurasia, and even the Middle East, we in the West don't have to think of ourselves as the saving force in world missions. This fact is underscored by the observation that knowledge of the gospel is growing in nearly every part of the world *but* the United States! This means, consciously for the first time, we now have the opportunity to learn from others as well as others learning from us. Can we learn something from Korea about prayer, from China about house churches, from Africa about discipleship? Mutuality reflects a shift from the one-up, one-down relationships stemming from a colonial approach to missions. Bishop Desmond Tutu made popular the observation that "when the missionaries came to Africa, they had the Bible and we had the land. They said, 'Let us pray.' We closed our eyes. When we opened them, we had the Bible and they had the land."[12] Hopefully, those days are behind us. Today there is a need for mutual respect and mutual learning. We from the West come not just to give but also to receive as true peers. And that's the challenge. As one mission's pastor said so well, "My biggest opportunity is to be a resourced, educated white guy and submit to a God-called foreigner who needs you."

Matt Olthoff, who in 2009 was serving as senior director for community development at Mariners Church in Irvine, California, noted in our conversation:

> There is a paradigm shift toward reciprocity that is taking place. What does it mean to come to the table as equals? The West is typically loud, directive, and the one that leads by bringing resources to the table. . . . Secondly, the church is growing in leaps and bounds in developing countries while the Western church is dying. We in the West have always been givers, but we need to learn to be receivers. Reciprocity is not about missions, but this is about the church in community.[13]

That openness led Olthoff and Mariners to hire Christian Mungai from Mavuno Church in Nairobi, Kenya, as their Global Outreach Pastor. Mungai then invited several pastors from Mariners to investigate firsthand what God was doing in Kenya. That visit served as a first domino that brought transformational change to Mariners Church. Within a few months, Mariners implemented a spiritual development program pioneered by Mavuno Church called "Mzizi," a Swahili word meaning "rooted." Today Rooted has been enthusiastically adopted by hundreds of churches around the country as their path to spiritual transformation. Rooted is built on "the integration of study, prayer, experiences, and relationships to accelerate life change because the participants are doing what they're learning while they are learning it."[14]

Scott White, pastor for global outreach at Lake Avenue Church, Pasadena, California, tells how he navigates in the new world of mutuality and partnerships:

I like to ask questions, listen, and learn because of the incredible challenge we in the Western church face in terms of humility. This past century has been our era of missions through the organizations like the IMB [the Southern Baptist Convention International Missions Board] and Campus Crusade [for Christ, now called Cru], but now we need new humility. In the past, partnership was us leading and you walking two steps behind us. In our post-Christian world, the opportunity to be a missional church is to learn from the missional churches overseas. They can teach us to be a pilgrim people. We can be their student as we have been their teacher. Models are not as transferable as before, but principles like humility, availability, and incarnational [ministry] are eternal. We have the opportunity to be blessed by them and learn from them if we are willing. Most of the training we have is for a different era. We need to think differently, or we will be confined to making missionary buggy whips.[15]

Tim Senff of Crossroads Church in Cincinnati, Ohio, unpacks what mutuality looks like in its partnership with Charity and Faith Mission Church in Mamelodi, South Africa, a township of a million people northeast of Pretoria. A few years ago, moved by the AIDS crisis in Africa, Crossroads stepped up to the plate by raising $750,000 to build a hospital in South Africa, providing free medical care for AIDS patients. Although the church led with a project, it followed up with relationships. "Relationships changed the game by knitting our hearts together, and this really changed us," says Tim. "We've had three big trips and have sent fourteen hundred Crossroads folks to Mamelodi, who spend the nights as guests in the homes of people in the township. This changes everything. No white people had ever done that before. Just as important, over one hundred people from Mamelodi have come to Cincinnati to help us accomplish our local mission. We do a pulpit exchange with our lead pastor, Brian Tome, exchanging pulpits with Mamelodi's Pastor Titus."[16]

Tim told us that the Mamelodi church had strengths and resources that Crossroads lacked. "They are so strong in prayer and pray for hours at a time. Recently we sent the church scores of Polaroid photos of ourselves along with our prayer request written in permanent marker on the front of the picture." Tim then showed me a picture of a Mamelodi woman, eyes closed with tears streaming down her cheeks, holding the picture of a young woman of college age with the prayer request that she would be 100 percent for Jesus. Welcome to the world of mutuality.

## Partnering

Partnering is different from mutuality. Mutuality is needed for true partnering to exist, but whereas mutuality has to do with the equality of those who come to the table, partnering pertains to the purposes or projects that require the need of real partners. Tom Mullis, then director for global outreach at Perimeter Church in Atlanta, points out that "the age of pioneering of Western mission is over, but many don't realize it. Local people are more effective in reaching local people. But they do need training. We in the West started as pioneers, but over the years, we have deteriorated into patrons of projects. Now we need partnerships around shared values rather than bringing in our separate agenda or program."[17]

Almost all the pastors I interviewed mentioned the absolute importance of long-term relationships as the singular key to sustainable and fruitful partnering. Matt Olthoff, of Mariners Church in Irvine, also shares a helpful insight on partnerships:

There is a big shift occurring now in missions. It's no longer ministry *to* or ministry *for* but ministry *with*. If you look at partnership from the West, it is very business-oriented and transactional. The rest of the world defines partnerships in terms of marriage—dating and courting—it's a relationship. We talk in terms of "transactional." They talk in terms of "communal." Our challenge is communicating reciprocity in greater means and measures.[18]

Bob Roberts, of Northwood Church for the Community, Keller, Texas, cogently sums up what is most needed. He advises churches, "Don't go in as the 'savior' but as a partner. Realize that you are going to receive as much from getting to know them and experiencing them as you will give them. Don't forget, you're a pilgrim, not a missionary. A missionary goes and gives with an end-game in mind or a project to complete. A pilgrim simply gives and receives on a journey."[19]

## Investing in Leaders

Leadership is everything. Wherever good things are happening, there will be a capable and passionate man or woman leading the way. Churches that are effective overseas have learned to invest in leaders. Keith West, pastor for missions at Lake Pointe Church in Rockwall, Texas, says:

We focus on a key leader of an indigenous church who shares our values and is getting the job done. We realized that if we came alongside these leaders, we could accelerate what they are doing so they could become a regional influence. It's like the parable of talents. We resource those who are doing the most with what they've been given and help them excel even more. We want to find a few key partners, stay with them, and pour into them to multiply their effectiveness.[20]

Similarly, Durwood Snead, director of GlobalX at North Point Church in Atlanta, says, "Our model is to work with indigenous leaders to help them develop, reproduce, and multiply from there. These multiplying churches then become models for other churches that become movements of churches."[21]

Eric Hanson, director of international impact at Christ Community Church in Saint Charles, Illinois, works with indigenous leaders who are doing church-planting multiplication in six countries around the world. He says, "We are doing things the hard way. It is easier for us to find a Western missionary who could integrate our people there, but we're led to indigenous leaders who have not been exposed to Western leaders. But we are seeing great fruit. We're always working uphill."[22] Since 2005, in Sierra Leone alone, they have seen over 1,100 churches started with over 40,000 new believers, and sense that God's spirit is pouring out on this work. Partnering with indigenous leaders does not mean a church doesn't send their own people, but the people they send are in service to the local leader.

How do you recognize good leaders who make great partners? The most obvious sign is that they are already engaged in ministry without any outside help. Steve Hanson, of the Church of the Open Door in Maple Grove, Minnesota, says, "When I go into a village, I don't know how to dig a well or build a building, but I do know relationships. When I walk into a local church in southern Uganda that is missing a roof because the people are using their monies to build houses for grandmothers to take care of AIDS orphans, I pay attention. They have a bigger God than I do."[23] For another pastor, God-sized goals distinguish one potential partner from another. "Our partner in northern India is working to plant five hundred churches in the next five years and a thousand churches before he dies."

## Combining Good Deeds and Good News

Externally focused churches, by definition, are churches that believe that the gospel is and has always been a message that is best expressed in both words of love and works of love. Good deeds verify the good news, and good news clarifies the good deeds.

Evangelistically, we believe that good deeds create goodwill, and goodwill is a great platform for sharing the good news. Combining good deeds and good news is not novel in foreign missions. This has always been a strength of the sending church—to add a component of physical blessing to the people it is trying to reach. Cinderblocks and paintbrushes fit neatly and comfortably alongside jungle mime and backyard Bible clubs in the toolbox of the short-term missionary. What is new is the level of problem-solving that externally focused missional churches are engaged in. What is new are the influential people who are speaking out for holistic global solutions.

In 2003, Saddleback Church's pastor, Rick Warren, was in Africa, where he had just finished a Purpose Driven Seminar that connected to 90,000 pastors on the continent. Afterward, he was taken to a remote village where he met a local pastor who faithfully downloaded Warren's sermons from Pastors.com at a post office ninety minutes away by foot. Meeting this obscure pastor proved both catalytic and providential as Warren began to pray about what he was to do with the influence God gave him. Under the African sky, Warren began to articulate the big "giants" facing humanity around the world. He came up with five global giants:

1. Spiritual emptiness. "[People] don't know God made them for a purpose."

2. Egocentric leadership. "The world is full of little [dictators]. Most people cannot handle power. It goes to their heads."

3. Poverty. "Half the world lives on less than $2 per day."

4. Disease. "We have billions of people dying from preventable disease. That's unconscionable."

5. Illiteracy. "Half the world is functionally illiterate."[24]

To take on the global giants, Warren came up with his PEACE Plan. As the Saddleback website explains, "The PEACE Plan is a massive effort to mobilize Christians around the world to address what Pastor Rick calls the 'five global giants' of spiritual emptiness, corrupt leadership, poverty, disease, and illiteracy by promoting reconciliation, equipping servant leaders, assisting the poor, caring for the sick, and educating the next generation."[25]

The goal of the PEACE Plan is to mobilize the body of Christ—the churches of the world—to engage the five big giants, and thousands of churches of all stripes are signing on to be a part of this global effort. Warren invites all comers: "We need to mobilize a billion Catholic and Orthodox believers. I'm really not that interested in interfaith dialogue. I am interested in interfaith projects. We do have different beliefs, but the fact is we serve the same Lord. Let's work on the things we can agree on."[26]

Today, churches are engaging the broken places of the world simply because these places are broken. "I like to ask people from developing countries what they think heaven will be like," says Steve Hanson of Church of the Open Door. "Most of them say, 'It will be a place where I don't need to worry about food and I won't hear my children cry because they are hungry.'" This is a far different view of heaven from most Westerners, who may view heaven as a mix between a nice beach and a country club. Having enough food doesn't even cross our minds. "'Give us this day our daily bread' is a prayer I've never had to pray," Hanson goes on to say. But for the two billion people on earth living on less than two dollars a day, this is their daily prayer, and the church has the opportunity to be an answer to that prayer.[27]

## Greater Financial Accountability

American churches are incredibly generous. "US church donations to both humanitarian and evangelistic transnational ministry now total about $4 billion annually."[28] However, churches that engage in global ministry are thinking differently about whom they support, what they support, and how they support missional engagement. One thing is clear: the days of cutting a check and hoping for the best are clearly over. With all the needs and opportunities in the world, global missions leaders of the future are trying to maximize every dollar expended on global outreach.

The paradigm of funding partnering is challenging. Mike Robinson, now retired from the position of stewardship pastor of Fellowship Bible Church in Little Rock, Arkansas, says, "Our challenge is to develop sustainable and healthy partnerships with indigenous people without enabling those who need help. When a 'gringo' walks through the door, local citizens see a dollar sign, which only leads to paternalism and dependence. The untold story is this: when Americans leave and take their money with them, the churches fold. All around the world, we see the skeletons of the great intentions of Americans."[29]

After ten years in East Asia, Jonathan Martin was invited to be the pastor for global outreach at Good Shepherd Community Church, Portland, Oregon. Living overseas as a supported missionary, he had seen the effects of well-intended but misplaced finances. This trail of financial havoc led him to ask, "How can we get behind indigenous works without destroying them? How can we be lavishly generous yet incredibly wise in our giving?" Meeting with a group of other like-minded leaders, Jonathan came up with four guiding principles that inform all the church's overseas giving decisions, summed up in the acronym *RAISE*:[30]

- R—*Relationship:* We cannot bypass relationships and must always lead with relationships—real, viable, and incarnational relationships. This is why we must have people on the ground, since money follows people.

- A—*Accountability:* Never give to an individual pastor or indigenous missionary. Give to organizations that provide oversight and accountability. Good people are ruined by easy access to money, no matter how well intentioned they are.

- IS—*Indigenous Sustainability:* This is all about helping locals do ministry without money. If it won't go on without Western money, we don't do it. Ask yourself: "Will the project I give to require ongoing and continual foreign funds to keep it alive, or are these funds seeding a plant that can eventually be watered and grown by locals?" If the project cannot be funded, maintained, and multiplied by locals, don't invest in it.

- E—*Equity:* We as Americans can create entities that destroy local life. If we build orphanages where children get better care and education than a parent can provide, parents will often bring their children to the orphanage. The financial gift should not create economic inequities in the place it is given. We may think, "This pastor shouldn't have to live in this shack. Let's build him a house." That may be the right thing to do, but we need to do so with the knowledge that his congregation may never learn to support that pastor financially. Why should it? "The Americans will cover for us and come to the rescue."

Greater financial accountability is a newly recognized reality that churches will need to navigate.

## Business as Mission

An emerging possibility for funding is attached to the effectiveness of business as mission. North Point's Durwood Snead explains:

> Our biggest challenge in missions is funding, and Business as Mission (BAM) is a new model for funding the mission. A well-run business will provide salaries for people doing business as mission. In an unreached world, business as mission is a big thing God has for this time in history. All countries desire economic development, so we're trying to figure out kingdom business. If we are employing people, we have great freedom to use the Bible as a management textbook to do this in countries closed to traditional missionaries. These are authentic businesses, and government welcomes them.[31]

Dave Hall of Emmanuel Faith Church, Escondido, California, says, "My challenge is figuring out how to maximize these entrepreneurs for the kingdom. Whereas before, the inroad was teaching English, now God is raising up a whole new group of people from the business domain. The traditional missionary who dabbles at something else will fade away, while professionals with kingdom mentality are the future."[32]

Joey Shaw, International Field Office director at Austin Stone Church in Austin, Texas, is trying to demystify global engagement and intentionally engage business-people in the church's ministry to Turkish Christians. "The energy we have here is for being global. We have a church full of what we call 'cosmocrats'—people who will fly overseas to attend a wedding or who regularly travel overseas for business. We are trying to make them cosmocrats for the kingdom." Desire is translated into strategy. Shaw describes:

> On our first trip to Turkey, in January 2008, I took a group of CEOs and businessmen. I did this intentionally to show that I wanted to engage the body beyond doctors and nurses. We investigated a business idea—a cheesecake factory. Interestingly enough, there is a market; Turks love cheesecake! Half the members of this team have developed business as mission, and they are now investors. Another group is looking to set up a Curves business in Istanbul. We are sitting on a gold mine of people to send, and we're racking our brains how to do this.[33]

Lake Avenue's Scott White notes that "as we become post-Christian, our funding model needs to be different. Much of our ministry's footprint is not sustainable the way it is. Most cultures around the world do not have a charity ethos regarding asking and giving, so most churches in these places don't ask and give. We must train in different ways to make bi-vocational funding the new norm of sustainability."[34]

So what's working in Business as Mission? In 2007 Mark Russell went to Chang Mai, Thailand, to discover what was working in the BAM world. He conducted 128 interviews and researched twelve BAM enterprises. The patterns began to emerge: BAM enterprises fell into two distinct categories—what Mark labeled "Blessing" enterprises and "Converting" enterprises. Blessing enterprises were characterized by

- a blessing orientation: "We're here to bless the people of Chang Mai" by creating jobs and making life better for them;

- an openness regarding purpose and identity: "We are followers of Jesus and we think this is how he wants us to help";

- partnership with local churches; and

- high cultural adaptation.

By contrast, the "Converting" enterprises had four different characteristics:

- a converting orientation;

- secrecy regarding purpose and identity;

- independence, preferring not to partner with others; and

- low cultural adaptation.

The evangelistic results of both approaches were startling. During the course of his research Mark discovered that the Blessing companies had seen forty-eight Thai individuals come to Christ while the Converting companies had, ironically, seen only one Thai come to faith.[35] It is the kindness of God that leads to repentance.

## Focus

There is power in focus. On the flip side, the most frustrated pastors interviewed were those whose churches supported scores of legacy missionaries they had inherited, scattered all over the map. Much of the time, these missionaries were not the home-grown variety but nephews of former staff, or friends of friends, or a missionary tied to a designated gift. In the past, the often-unstated goal of missions was to have representatives from the church on every continent of the globe. The more yarn and pictures, the better. This is changing. Churches that seem to be most effective in making a global impact are focused churches. When Neil Hendershot, missions pastor of Central Christian Church of the East Valley in Mesa, Arizona, was asked what the church was doing globally, he did not hesitate:

We are focused on holistic transformation through the expansion of the kingdom of God throughout northeastern Africa. We focus on unreached and unengaged people groups. Unreached people groups include those who may have an expression of Christianity but no church. An unengaged people group has no known believers with no one trying to reach it. Unengaged people will die without ever meeting a believer or hearing the gospel. All our efforts are along this focus.[36]

It doesn't take long to figure out what these folks do and don't do.

Ian Stevenson, serving in 2009 as missions pastor of The Crossing in Costa Mesa, California, said:

For us, the biggest thing is focus. A lot of churches have a full menu of stuff they keep adding to. We encourage individuals to go where they want to go, but as a church, we partner with five places to go and make a difference. Organizationally, we just do five. We have folks that go to France and a person in Zimbabwe, but as an organization, these efforts are not what we promote from the pulpit. For the sake of focus, we stick with our five partners.[37]

David Thoresen, director for international outreach at Pantano Christian Church in Tucson, Arizona, outlines the power of the church's dual focus:

Our focus is church-planting movements coupled with community transformation. We believe that wherever Jesus's church is present, lives and communities should be improved. God has brought us into relationship with some great indigenous partners who share our vision and passion that each church would have within its DNA the tools and desire to multiply itself. Wherever we plant churches, we want to transform communities, and clean water has been very big for us because it is tied to so many other areas of transformation. Our partner in India has started 750 churches, and our partner in Nigeria has planted over 400. Multiplying churches and transforming communities—that's what we're about.[38]

For Tim Senff, at Crossroads Church in Cincinnati, focus adds synergy to global engagement with Mamelodi, South Africa:

Our church loves to be able to focus our prayers, our thinking, our going, and our giving on one massive need in a specific location of the world. We've discovered the power of focus—going deep rather than wider. How we approach money, prayer, worship, and spiritual warfare is changed by focus. Our focus even caused us to change our mission from "Connecting seekers to a community of growing Christ-followers" to "Connecting seekers to a community of growing Christ-followers *who are changing the world.*" . . . People want to be part of a movement—a social force to change the world.[39]

## Technology

With every breakthrough in communication technology, people have made use of that technology to advance the gospel. The printing press, radio, TV, and the internet have increasingly allowed the church to enter a world without boundaries. All around us are churches that are discovering the power of technology—of having an impact in a country without ever physically visiting that country.

In 1993 Walt Wilson, a vice president at Computer Sciences Corporation (CSC), a $16 billion US corporation with six hundred offices overseas, was sent to the MIT Media Lab to figure out how the newly minted World Wide Web might "affect business around the world." Walt is a strategic thinker who has an eye for practical innovation. As the General Manager of Operations in the early years of Apple, Walt had worked closely with Steve Jobs on several projects, including the roll-out of the first Macintosh computer. Now with CSC, Walt was anxious to learn all he could about the internet. As a bright, strategic thinker and futurist, Walt immediately grasped the business potential of the internet, but as a follower of Jesus Christ, he had a fourfold question that would not go away:

If we had a connected global network . . .

- could we put God on it?
- could we connect to people who were searching for God?
- could we minister to people at their point of need?
- could we lead them to a relationship with Jesus and disciple them?

This was Walt's "Gutenberg moment." So, for the next few years he shared his question with prominent Christian leaders and funders around the country. Most of them smiled benignly, but no one took him seriously until he shared his vision with Paul Eshelman (of *Jesus* film fame) and Steve Douglass (president of Cru). They invited Walt to join the staff of Cru and figure it out together. And in 2004 Global Media Outreach (GMO) was born. Their BHAG vision, or Big Hairy Audacious Goal (a concept that originated with the *Good to Great* series of Jim Collins and Jerry Porras),[40] was "to give everyone on earth multiple opportunities to know and accept Jesus Christ, see hundreds of millions receive Him, build them in faith and connect them to the Christian community."[41] In November 2018, GMO announced that it had surpassed 1.8 billion gospel presentations and more than 200 million people had indicated decisions to follow Jesus, providing the hope of Jesus Christ to people in every country on earth. To see GMO's impact in real time, go to witnesstoall.com. It is impressive to see this technology in action!

GMO works from the premise that every day, millions of people around the world are searching for God and for purpose using the internet. Working with over 175 GMO partners, they have created over 150 websites that utilize key words a person might type in when looking for God or for answers in life—"Jesus?," "divorce," "marriage," "suicide"—or for popular activities like "world cup soccer" or "surfing." GMO then pays search engines like Google to ensure that seekers see one of the GMO websites first. So, if someone searches, "Who is Jesus?" the first site listed is usually a GMO site. Through the site they can find practical answers and understand how they can enter into a personal relationship with God through Jesus Christ. Thousands who trust Christ ask to be put in contact with another Christian. One of over five thousand online missionaries is then given the contact information, and the relationship begins through a secure server. To increase effectiveness, online missionaries can use templated letters and have access to gotquestions.com, whose tagline is "Your Questions. Biblical Answers," and has answers to more than 370,000 questions. Online missionaries allow GMO to remain highly personal and intentional with each individual. In fact, more than 750,000 individuals have maintained constant contact with their online missionary for more than a year.

Mike Neukum, director of missions at Bent Tree Church in Frisco, Texas, leads three online teams consisting of thirty-one online missionaries. Last year these stay-at-home missionaries responded to over nine thousand emails and saw 2,800 people indicate decisions for Christ. "Being able to correspond with people in closed countries, like Iran, is just something we are not going to do apart from the internet. GMO does such a great job with the templates and scripts that even a young believer can answer questions from Hindus and Muslims." GMO harnesses the best technology and the best people, blending high tech with high touch in order to introduce others to Jesus and help them grow. As one pastor noted, "It's like door-to-door evangelism except all of these people are knocking on your door."

Our changing world calls for a radical change in how we communicate in that world.

## The Leadership Challenge

Take a few minutes and review how your church is doing in terms of the eight big shifts of global missions. What might you do to improve your global impact?

| | GRADE | TO IMPROVE WE COULD... |
|---|---|---|
| MUTUALITY | | |
| PARTNERING | | |
| LEADERSHIP | | |
| EVANGELISM | | |
| FINANCES | | |
| BAM | | |
| FOCUS | | |
| TECHNOLOGY | | |

Figure 5.4

# 6.

# Partnering: They Build Wells, Not Walls

*If you want to go fast, go alone. If you want to go far, go together.*

—African proverb

Probably one of the most provocative statements and suggestions we made in our first book, *The Externally Focused Church*, was that the church could and should partner with any organization that is morally positive and spiritually neutral. Should churches serve alongside local community agencies or other churches with which they don't always agree? We continue to get more questions about "partnering" than just about any other topic. The partnership challenge is discussed, explored, and debated at almost every event we attend. We also hear some of the most inspiring and amazing stories from churches that jump into partnering with both feet—sometimes with very unlikely partners! We hope that the externally focused questions we've been asking of you to this point have been valuable. We hope that the questions we pose next will stir things up even more. What "partnership" questions you ask can make a world of difference to your scope of impact. Partnering and collaboration are not essential for becoming the best church *in* the community but are absolutely essential if you want to be the best church *for* the community.

## Two Concepts of Unity

In 1978, Paul Hiebert of Fuller Theological Seminary developed a construct that helps leaders think about whom they can and cannot align themselves with in their redemptive mission. Hiebert makes the distinction between a "bounded set" and a "centered set."[1]

### "Do You Believe What We Believe?"

Picture a bounded set as a circle. Inside the circle are various dots that signify the distinctive beliefs and practices of the "insiders" regarding the right way to baptize or the proper view of spiritual gifts or sacraments. It is this set of distinctive beliefs that determines who is in the group and who is outside the group. Traditionally, this is how denominations have defined themselves—by how they are

79

*different* from everyone else. When exploring the possibility of working together, the primary qualification of those in the bounded set is "Do you believe the same things we believe?"—and people are either inside or outside that circle (see figure 6.1). Some churches define their potential for partnership with other agencies or churches around that question. Thinking in a "bounded set" way, what is the size of the circle? How big—or rather how small—would our influence and impact be if we sought only partners who responded in the affirmative to "Do you believe what we believe?"

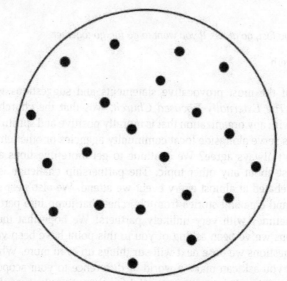

# Do you believe what we believe?

Figure 6.1

## "Do You Care About What We Care About?"

As Hiebert pointed out, there is another way to look at unity: through the eyes of a "centered set." A centered set consists of persons who share a common affection, interest, pursuit, or allegiance. The centered set can be depicted as a central dot representing Jesus, without any boundary determining who is "in" or who is "out."

Individual lives are depicted by arrows moving toward the center or away from it (see figure 6.2). This indicates that some people may be more or less passionate about or committed to the faith than others, but they are all directing themselves toward the same center. Hiebert even suggests that it is not distance from the center that is most important but the direction of the arrow. It is better to be far away and moving toward Jesus than to be next to Jesus but moving away.

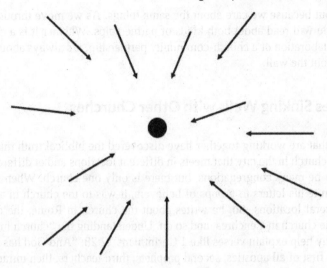

# Do you care about what we care about?

Figure 6.2

The centered-set diagram can also be adapted to change the conversation about who churches can work with. The dot in the center of the diagram can indicate any *cause* that the church or community cares about. We can work with anyone who cares about what we care about.

## Insight from Down Under

Missiologists Michael Frost and Alan Hirsch came up with a good illustration of the difference between a bounded set and a centered set:

> In some farming communities, the farmers might build fences around their properties to keep their livestock in and the livestock of neighboring farms out. This is a bounded set. . . . In our home in Australia . . . ranches are so vast that fences are superfluous. Under these conditions a farmer has to sink a bore and create a well, a precious water supply in the Outback. It is assumed that livestock, though they will stray, will never roam too far from the well, lest they die. This is a centered set.[2]

Churches that are transforming their communities think in terms of sinking wells rather than building walls. Theologically, the "well" is Jesus, of course, but the diagram also serves to define what people in the community mutually care about. Churches that are transforming communities don't divide over their differences but unite with other churches and community service organizations (faith-based or not) around their common love for the community. We can unite and work together with other churches and groups in our communities not because we share the same theology but because we care about the same things. As we move throughout this chapter, you will read about both kinds of partnerships. Whether it is a church-to-church collaboration or a church-community partnership, it's always about the well and not about the wall.

## Churches Sinking Wells with Other Churches

Churches that are working together have discovered the biblical truth that there is really one church in the city that meets in different locations and at different times. There may be many congregations, but there is only one church. When the apostle Paul wrote his letters to groups of believers, it was to the church in a city that met in several locations. So, he writes about the church in Rome, the church in Corinth, the church in Cenchrea, and so on. Understanding the "church in the city" concept may help explain verses like 1 Corinthians 12:28: "And God has placed in the church first of all apostles, second prophets, third teachers, then miracles, then gifts of healing, of helping, of guidance, and of different kinds of tongues."

As you look around your individual congregation, especially if yours is a small one, you won't necessarily see all those gifts, but you will certainly see them distributed across the whole church in the city. Understanding our congregations as parts of one larger church in the city allows us to experience the unity of family that we share in belonging to the same Father (Eph 4:3–6), the unity of fellowship as we accept one another and worship together (Rom 15:5–6), and the unity of purpose as independently or cooperatively we seek to let the world know that God sent Jesus and that God loves every person on earth as much as he loves his own Son (John 17:23). Congregations are discovering that sometimes we can publicly express our unity, not through parades or marches but through service that blesses our community.

It's no secret that people are walking away from church. Yet there is a glimmer of hope. Thirty-one percent of "lapsed Christians" report that they would be "more interested in Christianity if [they] saw various churches in [their] community working together more."[3] What could you do better with other churches than you can do by yourself?

### Catalytic Days of Service and Unity

In many communities around the country, churches are uniting around serving their communities for one- or two-day serving events. The advantage of such weekend events is that churches can jump-start their externally focused ministry by giving large numbers of people the opportunity to stick their toe in the water and get their feet wet in a well-planned, well-defined, time-bound opportunity that requires little preparation and training. This first experience is often the catalyst to deeper and more frequent engagement in serving others as people discover they are more fulfilled through contribution than consumption.

## Most Popular Ways to Partner with Other Churches

In 2006, Leadership Network conducted a survey with the nearly seventy churches involved in the Externally Focused Churches Leadership Communities. Church leaders were asked how they had partnered with other local churches in community service ministry. The following are the primary ways in which these churches have collaborated in community service:

- Food programs (food pantry, Meals on Wheels, and so on)
- Emergency assistance (providing food, clothing, or short-term financial assistance)
- Child and youth programs (tutoring, youth sports, and the like)
- Housing programs (Habitat for Humanity, homeless-shelter work)
- Prison ministry
- Medical and dental programs
- Immigrant ministries
- Special one-day project work

A couple of other interesting findings emerged. First, churches reported that they came together for prayer just as much as they gathered for community service work, and 96 percent of churches reported that "kingdom building" is their goal for working with other churches.[4] And one can expect this trend to accelerate. In May 2008, *Leadership Journal* surveyed nearly seven hundred evangelical pastors, asking "how their perceptions of the gospel and mission currently compare with their understanding a decade ago." Seventy-five percent of the respondents stated that partnering with other churches is essential to accomplishing their mission, compared to just 51 percent in 1998.[5]

One additional finding from the Leadership Network survey pertained to how churches in partnership measured the effectiveness of their collaborative efforts. Acknowledging the difficulty of measuring such effectiveness, and the need for improved metrics, the following list shows the most widely used forms of measuring success (survey participants could choose as many as applicable):

- Witness of unity to the community (71 percent)
- Total number of people served (52 percent)
- Total number of volunteers (52 percent)
- Number of new relationships formed (47 percent)
- Number of service events (31 percent)
- Number of first-time volunteers (33 percent)[6]

By asking "Do you care about what we care about?" we can head straight toward kingdom solutions to community and world problems. We partner not around our statements of faith or doctrine but rather around our common love for and commitment to our community.

## How Influence and Impact Can Grow

In the spring of 2004, leaders from my (Eric's) church, Calvary Bible Church of Boulder, Colorado, inspired by Little Rock's Sharefest, met with the superintendent of schools for the Boulder Valley School District and asked what they could do to help and serve. Church leaders said, "Give us the three schools that are in the worst shape, and we'll see what we can do." District officials identified an elementary school, a middle school, and a high school that were feeling the effects of budget cuts, time, and use. Seven hundred of the approximately one thousand people who attend Calvary Bible worked all day Saturday and three hours Sunday morning painting classrooms and hallways, scraping gum off of the undersides of desks and handrails, washing windows, striping parking lots, cleaning vents and sprinkler systems, landscaping and weeding, painting murals, and writing hundreds of letters of appreciation to the teachers and staff of these three schools.

The principal of the middle school beamed when she told me (Eric), "What you people have done today is an absolute miracle! You have accomplished more in a day than we could have done in three months." After cleaning the paintbrushes and storing the supplies, all of the volunteers met with school district officials at the high school for a celebration and barbecue. School officials were incredibly grateful for the $150,000 in labor and materials that were donated to the three schools. In tough economic times, that amount of money might mean that the music program, the art program, or another student opportunity won't be trimmed.

Once word got around, other Boulder area churches asked to come on board, so in 2005, fourteen hundred people from three churches did extreme makeovers at more schools. That year, church leaders and school leaders celebrated at Mackey Auditorium on the University of Colorado campus, followed by a catered barbecue on the sprawling lawn. School officials gushed in gratitude for the $212,000 the church had provided in service to these schools.

Year after year, under the talented leadership of local pastors and volunteers, Sharefest has grown. By 2009, so many churches and so many people had volunteered to serve in the 130 projects that Sharefest had to be spread to six different Saturdays as part of a "summer of service" that resulted in over $600,000 in benefits to more than thirty schools. Churches praying together and working together can make a huge difference.

## Who Else Cares? Sinking Wells with Others

Many local individuals and entities care about the community. This common ground of concern and care provides the opportunity to work with unlikely partners to achieve something greater than the church itself could do. People of good faith can partner with people of goodwill around things they commonly care about. So, you might ask, "Who else cares about under-performing schoolchildren?" or "Who cares about single moms or fatherless children?" We can build wells, not walls.

Rather than creating new faith-based entities, which take up kingdom resources, why not partner with others in the city who share a common concern for things you care about? Churches are finding tremendous leverage when they discover that partnering possibilities exist with almost any organization or entity that is morally positive and spiritually neutral. Working with groups outside our normal spheres puts us in face-to-face and shoulder-to-shoulder relationships that spawn a thousand unlikely conversations through which people come to faith. We need to tap into the power of cross-sector networks; it's about common care for the city.

Embracing the same sentiment, the venerable Christian statesman John Stott wrote in 1975, "God created man, who is my neighbor, a body-soul-in-community. Therefore, if we love our neighbor as God made him we must inevitably be concerned for his soul, body and community . . . and there is no reason why, in pursuing this quest, we should not join hands with all men of good will, even if they are not Christians."[7]

Most churches and leaders tend to think about creating new opportunities rather than partnering. It's almost a knee-jerk reaction. Let's suppose that Prairie Quest Church feels compelled to address an issue in its community—say, assisting the homeless (a huge need in any city). The typical path is to get a committee together to study the issue, appoint a task force, and set up a church homeless ministry. Needs are assessed, volunteers are recruited, money is spent, and we launch our effort to care for the homeless in our community. But are they reinventing the proverbial wheel, or using resources less effectively than they otherwise might?

It's likely that in your community someone is addressing homelessness at some level. The same is likely true regardless of the issue you wish to affect. Having participated with hundreds of churches in all kinds of communities, we can offer a lesson learned by accident: those agencies, groups, nonprofits, and government coalitions sometimes see the church as competition. Despite its efforts to do good, the church is often perceived as an enemy or as "too good" to collaborate with others.

In our local Colorado community, we have an excellent organization that addresses the homelessness issue. It's become a cooperative effort of churches, government, businesses, and nonprofits. The needs are assessed, volunteers are recruited, and the community comes together to address the issue. It isn't perfect, doesn't always lead to success, and requires a great deal of flexibility, but the church becomes part of the solution and engages in the conversation. People of good faith have come together with people of goodwill to work on problems they commonly care about.

## Street GRACE in Atlanta

In Atlanta, Unite! serves as a network of over 140 churches led by pastors and faith leaders from a wide variety of denominations and cultural and ethnic backgrounds who work and serve together throughout the city through unified prayer, along with deeds of kindness, mercy, compassion, and justice. Together they focus on four impact areas: justice, education, poverty, and families. One key initiative that came out of this coalition of churches was Street GRACE (Galvanizing Resources Against Child Exploitation; streetgrace.org). Atlanta is a major hub for child prostitution, and Street GRACE is working with churches, other faiths, social services, law enforcement, and government to eliminate the commercial sexual exploitation of children.

Of the unlikely partnership, Stephanie Davis, policy adviser on women's issues for Atlanta mayor Shirley Franklin, says, "Being a self-proclaimed feminist, I haven't had much chance to work with the far right . . . but the issue of commercial sexual exploitation of children creates an automatic response in any human being. No one has personal ownership of that issue."[8]

Unite! leader Chip Sweney says:

> It's pretty amazing. There have been people outside the church working on child exploitation for a few years, but they were running out of steam. This is a billion-dollar industry, and those in control won't give it up without a fight. We've come alongside them with fresh fighting power. We're not trying to dictate anything but just trying to be a player at the table and a good teammate. Going after this issue is a good example of multisector collaboration. The resources from the faith community have really helped. As Christ-followers, how can we not be involved in this and fight for these children? The small victories, such as fixing up homes for these children and getting kids off the street, have been really positive.[9]

## Season of Service in Portland

Imago Dei's Rick McKinley began the church not through Sunday worship but through selfless service to the people in the city center of Portland, Oregon. Each year, Imago provides hundreds of volunteers to spruce up several schools and provides hundreds of families with school supplies, clothing, food, and Christmas gifts. In 2007, the mayor of Portland gave Imago Dei the Spirit of Portland award for its work at six under-resourced schools in southeast Portland.[10] In the summer of 2008, the people of Imago Dei joined together with scores of Portland area churches and with the Luis Palau Association for a "summer of service" that culminated with a gift to the city of $100,000 for the benefit of homeless families and the education of recent high school dropouts. When the check was presented at a city council meeting in March 2009, Nick Fish, Portland's housing commissioner, made the following comment:

> Something has happened here that I think needs to be acknowledged. As long as I've lived in Portland, there has been . . . a divide between the faith community—particularly what I would call the more fundamentalist, evangelical wing of the faith community—and the city of Portland. It has been my impression that what has frequently been accentuated in that relationship is the differences. And there have been some people both in government and in the faith community . . . who have been very effective in emphasizing those differences, and we know it's easy to pick a fight and much harder to find common ground. . . . So I have watched this relationship evolve . . . with some skepticism, and I think this skepticism was shared by many in the faith community. But what has happened through this season of service has such a powerful resonance with all of us regardless of our faith or regardless of our path, that this has provided for us a new baseline for a new relationship of mutual understanding and respect. And "season of service," as I'm fond of saying, are three of the most beautiful words in the English language. If the season of service is a rose, we hope that it is a perennial and not an annual. And I'm so pleased with the Palau organization and Pastor Rick McKinley and all of the folks involved who have said this is going to be an annual event.[11]

## What Sustains Partnerships

Phill Butler, in his book *Well Connected*, defines a partnership as "any group of individuals or organizations, sharing a common interest, who regularly communicate, plan, and work together to achieve a common vision beyond the capacity of the individual partners."[12] People or entities don't partner together unless they really believe that they can accomplish more together than they can accomplish by themselves. And partnerships don't last unless each partner is gaining something from the relationship that they couldn't attain by themselves and seeing results that they would not be seeing working alone. The new thing God is doing is through unlikely partners working on common ground to achieve astonishing results.

## A Few Lessons Learned

LifeBridge Church of Longmont, Colorado, where I (Rick) serve, has established fifty-four partnerships in the community with school districts, social service agencies, government programs, nonprofits, other churches, local businesses, and community projects. Through the years, there have been plenty of lessons, much success, and a few failures. LifeBridge doesn't have any formal procedures for partnering but, rather, evaluates each opportunity based on its own strengths and weaknesses. The church has, however, discovered some informal guiding principles for the partnerships we take part in:

1. *Release Folks Outside the Walls*. We like to say, "It doesn't matter whether you are serving inside or outside the walls of the church as long

as you are serving." So, we list our internal ministry needs right alongside the community service opportunities and just count on good things to happen. We've discovered that somehow God does the math and people find their best place to serve. As long as they are honoring God and helping to meet needs in the church or the community, we're happy with that.

2. *Every Partnership Requires Understanding the Rules.* Every partnership needs defining boundaries and established communication channels. No matter how large or how small, each partnership has a LifeBridge "go-to" person. This person helps ensure that the church is doing what it said it would do and that the organization or other church is keeping its end of the deal. If there is a problem or if someone falls short or if more direction is needed, the LifeBridge liaison has the responsibility to communicate and help resolve the situation. The organizations we serve also have their rules. As much as I would love for our volunteers to be able to read Bible stories during a tutoring session, volunteers play by the rules and use the materials the school provides.

3. *You Don't Have to Wear the T-Shirt.* As a pastor, I want to see the church grow, and I care about getting the message of grace and hope to the community. One of my personal pet peeves, though, is when Christians do marketing and call it service. We have all seen the bottles of water given out at some community events that have the service times of the local church printed on them with Scripture about never being thirsty. I'm all for marketing, and there are ministries and activities that LifeBridge certainly wants to make the community aware of. But there are plenty of ways to market, and at LifeBridge, we prefer to keep marketing marketing and service service.

4. *Not Every Partnership Works Out.* LifeBridge has had times when the parameters of the organization it was connecting with simply weren't in line with things that the church valued, or when they posed moral issues that church leaders and volunteers couldn't live with. Other times, the organization's leadership changed and the new leaders didn't want to work with churches. There have also been times when LifeBridge was responsible for a failed partnership—when we honestly thought we could be of good use to a school or nonprofit but failed to do so. These times have provided some painful lessons for us. It is better to under-promise and then over-deliver, rather than vice versa—a lesson we learned the hard way on such occasions.

## Fellow Workers

The expression "fellow worker" is used twelve times in the apostle Paul's writings. Logically enough, Paul calls his Christian colleagues and friends Timothy, Mark, and Luke his "fellow workers," but this title is not reserved for professional Christians only. It is applied to Paul's partners from other parts of the community as well. The tentmakers Priscilla and Aquila are his fellow workers (Romans 16:3), as is Philemon, the businessman from Colossae, and Urbanus, perhaps a government official from Rome, along with a host of others. The expression "fellow worker" is a translation of the Greek word *synergos*, from which we get our English word *synergy*. Synergy implies that the whole is greater than the sum of the individual parts: 1 + 1 = >2. When we partner with others outside the walls of our church or ministry, synergy happens. We accomplish more together than we could ever accomplish alone. When synergy is present, we not only accomplish more but also become better people in the process. To become the best church *for* the community, we need to learn to work well and play well with others. Build wells—not walls.

## The Leadership Challenge

In the next ninety days, have lunch, coffee, or a break with six pastors in your city. If you are a pastor, you might initiate by saying something like this: "I feel a bit embarrassed that we've been ministering in the same town for all these years and yet haven't really sat down and talked. Could I take you to lunch?" While at lunch, you might ask the following questions: "Where have you seen God at work in our city?" "Where do you see the pain of the city?" "Is there anything God might have us do together that would make a bigger impact for the kingdom than we are presently doing by ourselves?"

In the ninety days after that, have lunch, coffee, or a break with six executive directors of human service agencies in your city. You might say something like this: "Hi, this is Pastor Harold Wong from Church of the Open Wallet here in the city. I know you've been serving the city for decades, and as a pastor, I am painfully aware of how little I know about what you great people do. Can I take you to lunch?" While at lunch, ask about the history and mission of the organization, and then ask, "What can we as a church do for you?" "As you were talking, I realized that you care about a lot of the same things we care about. Is there something we could do together?" "If we had twenty-five people available for four to six hours with no strings attached, how could we help you?"

In a third period of ninety days, do the same with school or government officials, asking these leaders to identify the biggest needs of the schools or city. In the fourth ninety days, have lunch, coffee, or a break with six leaders from the business world in your city—CEOs, company presidents, other executives. You might initiate by saying something like this: "What do you see as the biggest needs of our city?" "If you could change one thing about the future of our city, what would it be?" After listening and jotting down responses, you might say something like this: "Over the past year, I've been meeting with church leaders and leaders of government, schools, and nonprofits to try to identify the biggest needs of our community. Here's what we've come up with. I think we'd all agree that to solve these problems, it will take cooperation among all sectors of our community—the public sector (government), the private sector (business), and the social sector (human service agencies and churches). How can we work together to solve some of these issues?"

# 7.

## Systems: They Create Paradigms, Not Programs

*No good tree bears bad fruit, nor does a bad tree bear good fruit.*

—Luke 6:43

How does a church on an aisle slide over to a window seat? How does a church consistently engage in weight training rather than bodybuilding? How does a church become the kind of church that the community would not just miss, were it to leave, but would fight to have it stay? How does a church become both internally strong and externally focused? How does a church become the best church *for* the community?

The answers to these questions are found not in programs but in paradigms. A program has a beginning and an end. A paradigm is a pattern or model from which many programs and initiatives will flow, but they will emerge from your strengths, from your capacities and calling. This chapter, then, is about creating structures and systems that enhance, strengthen, and sustain externally focused ministry. This may be the most important chapter in this book. Leadership is not just about finding leaders but also about creating good systems. An average leader in a good system will produce more than a great leader in an average system.

Most churches say that service, mercy, and love for those outside the church are important aspects of the Christian life. But this chapter is not about what people say but about what people *do*. You must create structures that operationalize your values; otherwise, they are not really values—they are merely sentiments. For many Christ-followers, service and ministry are sentiments but not values. How can we make externally focused ministry a part of who we are, part of our DNA?

## Creating Structures for What We Value

Externally focused churches create systems that continually reinforce their values. To align our beliefs with our behaviors, we create structures for everything that we value in church. For example, if your church values the teaching and exposition of God's Word, you would never have a church service where the Word of God is not opened and read. Because you value prayer, you would never have a service where you did not pray. If you value the sacraments of baptism and the Lord's Supper, these are also regularly scheduled on your church calendar. Why do we structure these elements into the life of our church? At least partly because these are the very things that define us as a church, and to stop doing these things means that we stop being the church that God wants us to be. If we didn't open God's Word, we'd cease to be the church. If we stopped praying, we wouldn't be the church. So, we create systems and structures to help us live out our values and beliefs—and that's a good thing.

If we want the people we lead to "get into the game," we must create structures for them to engage. Systems and mechanisms are the link between our values and our behaviors. The right mechanisms cause good things to happen even when we are not paying attention to them. For example, if you have a system set up to pay your bills through some type of automatic transfer, think about how that simplifies your life. Somewhere around 2:00 a.m., while you are enjoying a good night's sleep, money is withdrawn from your checking account and your bill is marked "paid in full." The mechanism caused a good thing to happen even when you weren't paying attention.

In the book of Acts the Greek widows were being overlooked in the distribution of the groceries. This was a problem that was not going to go away. The early church leaders chose not to address this on a behavioral level ("You women should stop complaining; maybe a little fasting would do you good") but rather on the systems level. They instituted a mechanism—the diaconate—that would look out for the physical needs of the church, not just for that day, but for nearly two thousand years now. Good things have been happening even when no one was paying attention to them.

## What Would Jim Do?

Jim Collins, teacher, researcher, and writer, elevates systems even above strategy. In the *Harvard Business Review,* in an article titled "Turning Goals into Results," Collins writes:

Take 3M. For decades, its executives have dreamed of a constant flow of terrific new products. To achieve that end, in 1956, the company instituted a catalytic mechanism that is by now well known: scientists are urged to spend 15 percent of their time experimenting and inventing in the area of their own choice. No one is told what products to work on, just how much to work. And that loosening of controls has led to a stream of profitable innovations, from the famous Post-it Notes to less well-known examples. 3M's sales and earnings have increased more than 40-fold since instituting the 15 percent rule.[1]

Writing for *Inc.* magazine, in an article titled "The Most Creative Product Ever," Collins poses a question:

What was Thomas Edison's greatest invention? Not the light bulb. Not the phonograph. Not the telegraph. I agree with many Edison observers that his greatest invention was the modern research-and-development laboratory—a social invention. What was Henry Ford's greatest invention? Not the Model T but the first successful large-scale application of a new method of management—the assembly line—to the automobile industry. What was Walt Disney's greatest creation? Not Disneyland or Mickey Mouse but the Disney creative department, which to this day continues to generate ingenious ways to make people happy.[2]

## John Wesley and His System

Figure 7.1. William Hogarth, *Gin Lane* (engraving), 1751.

If we can borrow from a chapter in church history, the contrast between George Whitefield and John Wesley serves as an important lesson for us regarding the power of structures that affect behavior. England in the early 1700s was in an abysmal state—economically, socially, and spiritually. Many children began "at four or five years of age to work in the mines, the mills, and the brickyards. Fewer than one in twenty-five had any kind of schooling, and in 1736 every sixth house in London was licensed as a grogshop. This epidemic of drunkenness eroded what little decency was left among the working people, leaving them adrift in hopeless despair. The English populace was gripped in a vise of poverty, disease, and moral decay."[3]

I (Eric) was in London a couple of years ago, on an eight-hour layover between planes, so I took a taxi to the British Museum to have a look around. Among the fascinating displays was an exhibit of life in London in the 1700s. It was appalling. One engraving, *Gin Lane* by William Hogarth, depicted the times well. One woman is pouring gin into the mouth of her baby. Another woman is sprawled on a set of stairs, with a baby falling out of her arms to the street below. There is a man in front of a pawnshop gnawing a bone with his dog. Many people lie about, passed out. One man is being placed into a coffin, and another has taken his life by hanging. Hogarth was a social commentator, and he captured well the social and moral state of London. Into this hopeless environment stepped George Whitefield, who began what he called "field preaching." He was the finest preacher of his time. During a time when possibly only 1 percent of the British population was affiliated with the Anglican Church, Whitefield could draw crowds of several thousand coal diggers and mine workers. Even Benjamin Franklin sang his praises when Whitefield came to America. "Franklin calculated that Whitefield could easily address 30,000 people standing in an open place."[4]

Although it was Whitefield who popularized open-air mass evangelism, it was John Wesley who figured out how to preserve the fruits of such gatherings. Whitefield *hoped* that his converts would follow through on their decision, but Wesley, by contrast, created a method, or mechanism, to preserve the fruits. "He made sure that those who were serious about leading a new life were channeled into small groups for growth in discipleship. The class meeting [small group] turned out to be the primary means of bringing millions of England's most desperate people into the liberating discipline of the Christian faith."[5] Church historian Charles White notes that "'Methodists' were given that name because they methodically sought to obey the Lord in all areas of their lives by obeying three main rules:

- One, do no harm;

- Two, do as much good as you can; and

- Three, use all the means of grace that God has provided."[6]

Simply through converts participating in a small group and following these three basic rules, both their lives and society were dramatically improved: People abandoned sinful habits, like drunkenness, which had previously ruined their lives. By going to the Methodist meetings and following each word as they sang from the hymn book, they learned to read, which created upward mobility and better employment opportunities. And with a new view of money (Wesley's "Save as much as you can. Give as much as you can"), they created a large middle-class population.

After several years of ministry, near the end of his life, Whitefield lamented, "My brother Wesley acted wisely—the souls that were awakened under his ministry he joined in class and thus preserved the fruits of his labor. This I neglected, and my people are a rope of sand."[7] Such is the power of a catalytic mechanism.

Jim Collins says that good systems cause good things to happen even when no one is paying attention to them. That means that once Wesley's system of classrooms was in place, he could easily (or at least efficiently) oversee thousands of believers. One thing we are learning about systems is the place of small groups in externally focused ministry. If service outside the church becomes part of the DNA of every small group in a church, then the ministry of each small group takes on a life of its own. Without this, someone always has to be pushing programs. What if four to six times a year the elders or deacons took the first thirty minutes of the board meeting to take bags of groceries to single moms in the neighborhood? Imagine the stories they would have. What other externally focused systems could there be?

## Creating Systems That Influence Behavior

Externally focused churches are ones whose effectiveness is not measured merely by attendance but also by the transformational effect they are having on the community around them. They share the gospel in word and deed; otherwise, for them, it's really not the gospel. How does a church build external focus into its DNA? We'd like to suggest six things any church can do to scoot from the aisle seat to the window seat. These are six different practices that externally focused churches consistently engage in to extend and reinforce who they are and strive to be. These are the vital signs and benchmarks of externally focused ministry.

### Start with a Strong Scriptural Foundation

Fundamental to an externally focused church is a strong theological foundation. To use a coaching analogy, the foundation consists of the basic skills of a sport that must be mastered before players can begin improvising. When God first began giving guidelines and statutes to people, such commandments included laws on justice and mercy. So as early as Exodus 22, God gives guidance for just and merciful compassion toward the poor, widows, orphans, and strangers. In the books of Leviticus and Deuteronomy, God, through Moses, is more specific in how all people should be treated, regardless of their physical condition or social status. The teachings are clear. One author and practitioner noted that injustice was "the second most prominent theme in the . . . Old Testament—the first was idolatry. [Additionally,] one out of every sixteen verses in the New Testament is about the poor or the subject of money."[8]

What then should you do? Saturate yourself in the Gospels. As we asked in chapter 4, what did Jesus do? Christology (the life and teachings of Jesus) informs and shapes our missiology (our understanding of what the mission of the church should be). Missiology then shapes and guides our ecclesiology—how we structure church to accomplish our God-given mission. Many churches start with the usual mission, vision, purpose, values, and exercises and then illustrate them from the life of Jesus or the book of Acts. But all mission is really rooted in and begins with the mission of Jesus.

In 1984, a small leadership team at Mariners Church in southern California spent an entire year immersed in the study of God's Word, endeavoring to discover what God had to say about the poor and those in need in the community. These leaders were startled to find out how much God had to say about caring for the poor, widows, strangers, and orphans that God has placed around us. References to helping people in need were found in both the Old Testament and the New. It took them aback to see how directly God spoke about how the poor should be treated and what is expected of the church in fulfilling the needs of the poor. The church leaders felt a burden to heed God's direction and accept the responsibility to bring their findings to their bourgeoning church of four hundred members. It was time to take action. It was time to take the field. Their theology informed their vision: "The vision of Mariners Local Outreach is to help every poor and needy person in Orange County. We want to bring God's kingdom to these people by sharing through word and deed the message of the Gospel." The vision then shaped their threefold goal: "First, we teach our members what the Bible has to say about serving those in need. Second, we encourage them to become personally involved. And finally, we provide opportunities to serve."[9] As the leadership team brought its findings to the congregation, the congregation enthusiastically responded, with one-fourth of the members signing up to be involved and donating $12,000 to jump-start what would become Lighthouse Ministries.

Today, Mariners Outreach, as it is now called, has an externally focused budget of nearly $4 million. Each year, thousands of Mariners' people give of themselves in service to others—working in after-school programs on Minnie Street in neighboring Santa Ana, or mentoring moms who permanently live in motels as part of the Miracles in Motion ministry. Because love, compassion, and service are "who they are," when Hurricanes Katrina and Rita struck in fall 2005, Mariners bought vans (that later would be donated to Gulf Coast churches) and mobilized scores of rotating teams to clean up and help rebuild lives and homes in the devastated areas. It's who they are; they could do no less. And in addition to sending helpers, special offerings allowed them to donate tens of thousands of dollars. It's who they are; they could do no less. To the people of Mariners, externally focused ministry is not a program or an emphasis. It is who they are, and to stop serving, giving, and loving would jeopardize their very existence. Today their mission is to "inspire people to follow Jesus and fearlessly change the world." Their vision is "a movement of disciple-making churches changing the world." Each of their church plants passes on the DNA of Mariners by having a community center embedded into the church property. But it all began by looking at the heart of God in the Scriptures.

## Preach About It Regularly

Build God's heart into the rhythms of your preaching and teaching regarding those on the margins of society and the absolute need for service and ministry as it pertains to our own spiritual growth. The message of good news and good deeds resonates not only with believers but with seekers and nonbelievers as well. A strong theological base forms the foundation for implementing every other strategy. The Scriptures are rich with God's heart for the less fortunate. Jesus's first public words, when he explains the purpose of his ministry in the Gospel of Luke (4:18–19), are from Isaiah 61:

> The Spirit of the Lord is on me,
> because he has anointed me
> to proclaim good news to the poor.
> He has sent me to proclaim freedom for the prisoners
> and recovery of sight for the blind,
> to set the oppressed free,
> to proclaim the year of the Lord's favor.

Jesus's kingdom mission was to be one of good news and good deeds—combining words of truth with works of grace. Of course, Jesus loved and nurtured those who were closest to him (John 13:1), but he was always going after what he didn't have, not just preserving what he did have. He spoke about the shepherd who was willing to "leave the ninety-nine [sheep] in the open country and go after the lost sheep until he [found] it" (Luke 15:4). When pressed to stay in a place where he was appreciated and lauded, "Jesus replied, 'Let us go somewhere else—to the nearby villages—so I can preach there also. That is why I have come'" (Mark 1:38). Jesus taught about loving one's neighbor by telling the story of the good Samaritan (Luke 10:25–37). He explained that one day God would judge our truest spiritual condition by how we treated those most unlike us—the hungry, the thirsty, the prisoner, the sick, and the stranger—and he punctuated his message by saying, "Truly I tell you, whatever you did for one of the least of these brothers and sisters of mine, you did for me" (Matt 25:40). The early disciples were so captivated by the teachings of Jesus that they too lived them out. Paul was eager to help the poor (Gal 2:10), and James was concerned that the poor be elevated to honor (Jas 2:1–13). The first decision the early church made regarded the care of widows (Acts 6:1–7). The disciples fully grasped the teachings of Jesus.

One of the responsibilities of leaders is to communicate vision. There was a time when I (Rick) taught that vision was a clear, compelling magnetic image of a preferable future. It was something I'd read or heard, and it sounded good. After a few decades, however, I realized that vision is a glimpse of the future, and every time it goes by, a bit more becomes clear. As leaders, it is our job to help communicate the vision we see, and that means we must tell the story, tell the story, tell the story. Rick Warren is right: we preach to a parade. We can never share the vision too much.

A few years ago I (Rick) preached through the Gospels for the entire year. The series was called "A Year with Jesus." As you can imagine, this provided regular opportunities to speak of being externally focused. Truth is, there is so much in the Scriptures about caring for those around us that it isn't too tough to have externally focused language be a part of any message or series.

Like so many other congregations, LifeBridge has developed some additional sites. There are currently two venues in different towns within half an hour of the main LifeBridge campus. Both of these venues use video as a primary way of presenting the message. Our campus pastors do a great job of making sure that we get their part of the body serving in their own, unique communities. In fact, before either site launched, we led with months of serving. This set the stage for an external focus from day one of these new communities of faith. Campus pastors and lead volunteers connected with the local police and government officials to learn what needs existed. The first partnership and service opportunities in those venues came with the schools LifeBridge rented on weekends to hold worship in.

No matter what campus you visit, LifeBridge is big on sharing stories. The best way to communicate vision is storytelling: stories of people serving and people being served, and how God is using each of us to make a difference. Everyone has a story, and LifeBridge has created systems to collect and share them as often as possible.

## Make It Part of Your Plans

Many large churches have an "executive pastor"—a fancy title bestowed in exchange for doing what the senior pastor didn't want to do: hire staff, do performance reviews, plan, evaluate, and so on. Regardless of whether your church has such a position, every church has someone who aligns people and resources to serve the mission. The big idea here is that every person, program, or financial resource that is not helping further the mission is, by definition, a waste of resources. Most churches have a planning cycle in which each ministry leader or volunteer is asked to submit plans for the next cycle of ministry (quarter, semester, or year). If we want to maximize the opportunities to get everyone in the game, we need to think of creative strategies to engage everyone in externally focused ministry. Because we staff and budget around what we value, in every planning cycle each ministry department, from children to senior adults, can be asked to submit a plan for what they will do to get their people ministering and serving outside the walls of the church. Structures and systems help transform values and intentions into reality. Because we want to build ministry and service into the life of our church and into the life of every person, we need systems that help bring that about. If our values and objectives are right and the behavior is lacking, the problem is normally that there are no systems in place that operationalize the values and influence behaviors and habits. Programs and tactics are what help people live out and experience the values of the church.

## Engage in Regular Church-Wide Days of Service

Provide opportunities for those who are not part of a small group or age-segmented ministry: regularly scheduled church-wide community projects help everyone get into the game. Every church could provide an annual day or weekend when everyone can participate in a community service project. Such projects don't require previous screening and can include the contribution of people of all ages—from babies in backpacks to senior adults. This is an opportunity for parents and grandparents to serve alongside their kids and grandkids. Having experienced these types of events in our own churches and having heard countless stories from other churches, we see the value of children working alongside their elders as they together seek to be Christ-followers in practical ways.

Having an annual service event is a great way to encourage intergenerational service. Wouldn't it be great to serve together year after year? Research shows that many young people walk away from their faith after high school. Wouldn't it be great if we could raise up a generation whose testimony might be something like this: "When I graduated high school, I tried to walk away from the faith, but I couldn't get over the reality of the good that my family and my church did in the community." Faith content may vary from young person to young person, but the church can definitely model what it means to live life as a giver and not just a taker.

## Think Kingdom, Not Church

In externally focused ministry, you will do many things that help people in your community experience life closer to how God intended it, but these ministries may never directly benefit the numerical growth of your church. If you are using love and service to others as tactics to get a bigger crowd, you will probably not achieve that goal. People can sniff out ulterior motives a mile away. Through your externally focused ministry, people will come to know Jesus, but they may join someone else's church. You may raise up an army of servant-leaders that will serve in other places besides your church. But that's probably okay. When we meet Jesus face-to-face, the questions he will likely ask us will be more about how well we loved than how big our church was.

## Infuse Service into Small Groups

John Wesley always viewed service and ministry to others as an integral part of his "class meetings" of small groups, home groups, and community groups. Interestingly, he was greatly influenced by a French Catholic nobleman from a century before, Gaston Jean Baptiste de Renty. de Renty dedicated "his whole life to caring for the poor and encouraging his countrymen to a devout and holy life." Among the practices Wesley took from de Renty and incorporated into his small groups was "the establishment of little gatherings of devout people who met weekly for prayer, reading devotional books, distribution of food to the poor, and discussion of personal religious experience."[10] Wesley did not use his small groups for personal Bible study. He felt people got all the Bible they needed to act on during the weekly gathering of the church. Again, following de Renty's belief that personal and spiritual growth came through service to others rather than careful attention to and introspection of self, Wesley put thousands on the playing field.

A system to get people into the game is to infuse service and ministry to others into the life of every small group, as Wesley did. Ensure that every small group that is started has regular engagement in ministry or service outside the church or the small group. For churches that employ this tactic, service and ministry are just part of what it means to be in a small group. For most benchwarming small groups, the biggest challenge is "What should we study next? A topical study? A book of the Bible? Some book by Tim Keller?" By infusing service and ministry into the life of every small group, the questions become more interesting: "What good should thrive in our community because of this small group? What evil should die in our community because this small group exists? What will be different in the world a year from now because of this small group?"

Service not only benefits others and helps us grow as believers but also builds community among the members of a group. One externally focused pastor put it this way: "Community is like sweat: it happens when you work."

## Chase Oaks Church

Chase Oaks Church Plano, Texas, has been known for its internal health since its inception forty years ago, but in 2005 the actual DNA of the church was changed when Small Groups Pastor Glen Brechner called all the small group leaders together for a meeting and summarily fired every one of them—but then rehired all of them before they left for the evening. Their old job was leading a weekly or biweekly home Bible study. That job no longer existed. Going forward, Glen was asking each small group to have an external focus.

"It's been absolutely electric," Glen says. Each group now commits to an externally focused ministry for one year and develops relationships with the people the group members are serving and working alongside. The expectation is that every fourth or fifth meeting, the group forgoes chips and dip for serving in its compassion ministry. "This has lit our people up," says Glen. With over sixteen hundred adults in eighty small groups, that's a lot of ministry taking place each year.

What is different now about Chase Oaks Church? For one thing, what's "normal" at church is different at Chase Oaks. With an abundance of churches in the Dallas area, people in the community have plenty of options for their church experience. People come to Chase Oaks because the church is active in the community. One man put it this way: "I don't know why I'm here in church, but last week you guys painted my neighbor's house, and I thought, 'I should check this church out.'"[11] Second, a new group of leaders have emerged at Chase Oaks. Previously, most folks thought one needed to be a Bible teacher to be a small-group leader, but now leaders tend to be more entrepreneurial. Each Life Group has four leadership positions:

- The group leader, who gets things organized

- A "connect champion," responsible for creating community within the Life Group

- A "growth champion," responsible for biblical content

- A "bridge champion," who leads the Life Group into making a difference in the community

The structure, depicted in figure 7.2, is simple. Each Life Group has three goals: connect relationally, grow spiritually, and make a difference—belong, believe, and bless.

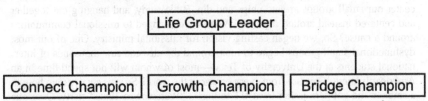

Figure 7.2

What are the other benefits of externally focused small groups? Here are a few things that we've discovered along the way:

### Small Groups Help People Live on Mission

You're already familiar with our belief that good deeds create goodwill and that goodwill is a wonderful platform for sharing the good news. But something must come first. It is good friends who help turn good intentions into good deeds, which in turn creates goodwill, which leads to opportunities to share good news. What we've found is that as much as we'd love for every individual to be living out their Ephesians 2:10 calling, it is service with our friends that is the critical path to get there. We've discovered that people are more likely to do something they don't really enjoy doing with people they like being with than they are to discover that place of service by themselves.

Volunteer guru Don Simmons reminds us that "93 percent of North Americans are not self-initiators, so we really can't say, 'Here I am; send me.' Rather we must say, 'Here we are; send us.'"[12] Serving with others you like being with is a greater motivator than just discovering your spiritual gifts. Sometimes when I (Eric) am speaking, I will say to the audience, "If after taking a spiritual-gifts test and being exhorted to find your place of service, if you actually went and did something, please raise your hand." Of the hundreds of people to whom I've asked that question, only one woman in Canada raised her hand—and it turned out that she was only stretching.

## Missional Small Groups Create Community

Community is a by-product of something greater. Speaking at a Leadership Network conference in Dallas in 2009, Matt Carter, lead pastor at Austin Stone Community Church, told of the Stone's journey into missional small groups:

> As much as we tried to build community through community groups, we had to admit that we stunk at building community. Most were inwardly focused and had trouble getting along with each other. We had to ask ourselves, "What is it in life that forms authentic community?" Our answer was "mission." That was the "aha" moment for us. Isn't that how Jesus built community? "Follow me and I will make you a fisher of [people]." We took that principle and applied it to our small groups. What if we didn't center our small groups around chips and dip, Bible study, and hanging out together and centered instead around mission? What if we changed to missional communities around a cause? So, we began casting vision for missional ministry. One of our most dysfunctional small groups began to look around the city and saw thousands of international students at the University of Texas—most of whom will not spend time in an American's home. They are from every corner of the world. So, this small group bought a smoker and got permission from UT to host a "Welcome to Texas" party. Over one thousand international students showed up, ate barbecue, and square-danced. This was step one. Then the group asked, "How do we engage them in the gospel?" So, they gathered other missional communities and began to recruit them to other events. Now families from other communities adopted these students to have dinner, do laundry, and have conversations about Jesus. It has made such a difference. Here is the crazy thing. If you were to go to this small group, what was once ugly, dysfunctional, and asking, "How are you going to meet my needs tonight?"—you now have a group that is walking in mission together, loving, walking, and serving together. It's happening all over our church. We have over three hundred missional communities. Now here's the thing: when we aimed simply for community, we got neither community nor mission. When we aimed for mission, we got mission and community almost every single time.[13]

Writing about social movements in his book *The True Believer*, Eric Hoffer addresses the importance of action, not thought, as the catalyst that brings people together:

> Action is a unifier. There is less individual distinctness in the genuine [person] of action—the builder, soldier, sportsman and even the scientist—than in the thinker or in one whose creativeness flows from communion with the self. Those who came to this country to act (to make money) were more quickly and thoroughly Americanized than those who came to realize some lofty ideal. The former felt an immediate kinship with the millions absorbed in the same pursuit. It was as if they were joining a brotherhood. [People] of thought seldom work well together whereas between [people] of action there is usually an easy camaraderie. Teamwork is rare in intellectual or artistic

undertakings but common and almost indispensable among [people] of action. The cry "Go, let us build us a city, and a tower" is always a call for united action"[14]

## Externally Focused Groups Really Help People

Missional communities have sufficient critical mass to make a sustainable difference. In 2008, Rick and I were in Alor Star, Malaysia, meeting with pastors and talking about externally focused ministry and the potential of small groups as the most underleveraged resource for externally focused ministry. In Malaysia, most churches work from a "cell group" model, and without a mission, even the best cell groups can turn inward. When I returned to the country six months later, Pastor Kuilan of Trinity Baptist Church in Alor Star asked me to lunch. He explained that after the first conference, he had returned to his church and asked all the cell group leaders to begin loving and giving themselves to others who could do nothing for them in return. They threw themselves into the mission. Pastor Kuilan then brought out a three-ring binder and leafed through page after page of pictures and stories of what the cell groups had done. Some had adopted single moms; others, disabled children and adults. Others served in an apartment complex, and some worked with orphans. Serving others had totally transformed the church, but even more important, the church was really making a difference in the community.

We believe that small groups are the very best way to help a church live out its externally focused, missional DNA. Imagine what your church would be like and the impact you'd have on your community if every small group served and loved the city? What new kingdom good would thrive? What would it be like if every few weeks, instead of three hours of hospitality, snacks, Bible study, and prayer, the small group acted to meet the needs of something God cares about in the world? When small groups become missional, the church changes and a small patch of the world is changed. You've become the best church you can be *for* the community.

## The Leadership Challenge

Using figure 7.3, rate your church's commitment and progress in the following basic areas of externally focused ministry (EFM) by circling the number that most accurately reflects the church's current circumstances.

What is your score? If you found yourself circling 4s and 5s, you were most likely reflecting the externally focused nature of your ministry. If you averaged 3 or below, you know you have lots of potential for growth. What areas are within your power to influence or correct? Make it your goal to move up at least one number in those areas in the next three to six months.

| | 1 | 2 | 3 | 4 | 5 | |
|---|---|---|---|---|---|---|
| No Scriptural Understanding | 1 | 2 | 3 | 4 | 5 | Strong Scriptural Foundation |
| No Preaching About EFM | 1 | 2 | 3 | 4 | 5 | Regular Preaching About EFM |
| EFM Not Reflected in Plans | 1 | 2 | 3 | 4 | 5 | EFM Integrated Into All Plans |
| No Church-wide EFM Projects | 1 | 2 | 3 | 4 | 5 | Regular EFM Church-wide Projects |
| Thinking Our Church over God's Kingdom | 1 | 2 | 3 | 4 | 5 | Thinking God's Kingdom Over Our Church |
| No Scriptural Understanding | 1 | 2 | 3 | 4 | 5 | Strong Scriptural Foundation |

Figure 7.3

# 8.

# Evangelism: They Deploy Kingdom Laborers, Not Just Community Volunteers

*The harvest is plentiful but the workers are few. Ask the Lord of the harvest, therefore, to send out workers into his harvest field.*

—Matthew 9:37–38

A couple of years ago, I (Eric) was meeting with a number of externally focused church leaders. They were engaged in creative exercises and brainstorming around the topic of volunteers and how to get more people engaged in purposeful service and ministry in the community. The discussion of externally focused leaders was progressing nicely when one of the leaders asked a perceptive question: "When Jesus asked us to pray for laborers for the harvest field, is putting more volunteers in the community the answer to his prayer for laborers?" Wow! What a zinger! Jesus didn't ask us to pray for volunteers for the community but to ask him for workers for the harvest field.

The group divided into a number of working groups where volunteers in the community and workers in the harvest were compared and contrasted. And finally it was concluded that *a volunteer in the community becomes a laborer in the harvest field when they combine the good news with the good deeds.* Wow! Now that is a big idea that we can attach ourselves to.

Please don't misunderstand our point. We want to say from the outset that the world needs multiple times more compassionate, good-hearted volunteers. They are the instruments of God's common grace in the redemptive process. But we also want to make a distinction between community volunteers and kingdom workers. Kingdom workers always have an eye for introducing people to the King. They are convinced that real and abundant life is found in a relationship with the living God.

## The Ministry of Jesus: Good News and Good Deeds

When the apostle Peter preached the good news for the first time to a group of non-Jewish people, he chose to summarize Jesus's ministry in a few short sentences found in Acts 10:36–38: "You know the message God sent to the people of Israel, announcing the good news of peace through Jesus Christ, who is Lord of all . . . [and] how God anointed Jesus of Nazareth with the Holy Spirit and power, and how he went around doing good." All that Jesus did was summarized in good news and good deeds. First, let's look at how Jesus went about doing good.

## Ministry of Mercy

First, Jesus did good through his ministry of mercy. Mercy is God's attitude and action toward people in distress. Mercy is distributed without qualification. Or, if there is a "qualification" at all, it is not people's worthiness but their distress. Like grace, mercy can be neither merited nor earned. When received, mercy makes someone's life better, if only for a day. Mercy is expressed in giving people a fish so they can feed themselves for a day. When Jesus fed the five thousand and when he fed the four thousand, he gave them the loaves and fishes not because they were worthy but because they were hungry. "I have compassion for these people; they have already been with me three days and have nothing to eat. I do not want to send them away hungry, or they may collapse on the way" (Matt 15:32). Notice that Jesus wasn't fearful that people would die but that people might collapse or faint along the way. So, after multiplying the loaves and fishes, he sent them on their way.

Now if they were like many of us, they'd probably be hungry again when they got home. This act of mercy did not cure world hunger. Jesus didn't take a systemic approach to their hunger by giving them tips on reaping a bigger harvest or seed-planting techniques. He also didn't shame them by saying, "You should have known that this was going to be a long time of teaching, and you should have brought your own food, so to teach you all a lesson, I'm sending you home without any supper." No, he multiplied the food, and everyone had more than enough. That's what mercy is; that's what mercy does.

Think of when Jesus and his disciples stopped by the home of Peter and Andrew. Most likely Peter said something like this: "Hey, we're pretty near my house. I'll bet my mother-in-law will whip us up a good meal if we hurry." So, the text says, "When Jesus came into Peter's house, he saw Peter's mother-in-law lying in bed with a fever. He touched her hand and the fever left her, and she got up and began to wait on him" (Matt 8:14–15). Peter's mother-in-law probably had many fevers in her lifetime and would probably have many more to come, but for that evening, Jesus made her life better. That's what mercy does. So, she whipped up a spesh and had a great evening of fellowship with Jesus, her son-in-law, and his buddies.

Mercy is expressed in the deeds of the good Samaritan (Luke 10:25–37). Where others had passed the bruised and beaten man, the Samaritan saw him, went to him, bandaged his wounds, put him on his donkey, took him to the inn, spent the night with him, and paid the innkeeper in the morning with the promise to cover any additional expenses. Mercy is as simple as medical help, transportation, companionship, lodging, and perhaps a little well-spent cash.

My (Eric's) son Andy, along with his wife, Natalie, and their three children, have lived in China for the past sixteen years, sharing their faith in Christ and building spiritual movements on college campuses. A while back Andy told me that before he does Bible study each week with groups of students, they go into the streets and serve the poor and the migrants. When I asked him how he decided to do this, here's how he replied: "Dad, remember how Jesus ends the parable of the good Samaritan? He says, 'Go and do likewise'—not 'Go and *think* likewise' or 'Go and *value* likewise.' It's our goal to help students become like Jesus, and I can't tell if they are becoming like Jesus by the answers they give me in Bible study, but I can tell if they are becoming more like Jesus when they serve and love as Jesus did."

Churches have figured out that mercy is a wonderful expression of what it means to be like Jesus to the world. Sometimes you may wonder, "With all the need in the world, what difference could we possibly make?" Perhaps you have heard the story of the boy walking along the beach with his father. A recent storm had washed thousands of starfish up onto the beach, and many of them were dying. The boy began stooping over and tossing the starfish back into the surf. The father, somewhat puzzled, asked his son, "With the thousands of dying starfish stranded here on the beach, what difference do you think you can make?" Without breaking stride, the young boy picked up another starfish, lobbed it into the sea, and said, "Well, Dad, I just made a difference for that one"—he tossed another—"and for that one"—he tossed another—"and for that one." Mercy is about making a difference for "that one."

If you are wondering where you might get started in your ministry of mercy, turn to Matthew 25:31–46 and review the story of the sheep and the goats. In this passage, Jesus commends people for how they responded to the hungry, the thirsty, the unclothed, the sick, the stranger, and the prisoner. Being merciful is as simple as providing food, clean water, clothing, medical attention, hospitality, or visitation to people in distress.

One day I (Eric) received an email from a Leadership Network coworker who had just returned from Healing Place Church (HPC) in Baton Rouge, Louisiana. He wrote:

> I'm just finishing up a great trip to Healing Place Church (HPC) in Baton Rouge. Healing Place is not a place to go if you want to play church. The congregation is committed to reaching out to hurting and poor people in the area. For example, yesterday, our group took a 40-minute trip over to the Donaldsonville Campus to visit and feed the widows. I'm quite embarrassed to say that this was my first experience actually doing something that God commands us specifically to do. Each Thursday, HPC feeds close to 70 widows in this small, very poor community (the average income in this neighborhood is just $8,900 per *year*). At each house, we went in and prayed with these women and gave them something to eat. These are people that the world has forgotten, but [that] HPC is ministering to. And you should have seen how much these women appreciated the visit. A lot of ministry took place in those two short hours. It stretched me and was a great experience. This type of ministry goes on each and every day here at Healing Place. Last year alone, they gave over $1 million to missions and outreach, prepared 65,000 meals for hungry people, provided medical care to 1,300 people, made 1,200 hospital visits, gave away 1,800 $25 Christmas vouchers to under-resourced people, and saw over 1,400 people make first-time decisions for Christ.[1]

## Ministry of Empowerment

Jesus went about doing good not just through his ministry of mercy but also through his ministry of empowerment—Jesus's healing ministry. Anytime Jesus healed someone of a debilitating disease or caused the deaf to hear, the blind to see, or the lame to walk, he was improving the recipient's life not just for a day but for the rest of the person's life. He was helping people move from dependency (most of these people had to beg in order to survive) to sufficiency.

After reading Psalm 68:5, "A father to the fatherless, a defender of widows, is God in his holy dwelling," Pastor Robert Gelinas of Colorado Community Church in Aurora, Colorado, asked himself, "If God is the father to the fatherless, who is the mother to the fatherless?" His answer was "the bride of Christ, the church." As a cofounder of Project 1.27 (project127.com), Robert is excited to see the results of this way of empowering children. Working with other Colorado churches, as well as governmental and other organizations, Project 1.27 has found permanent families for hundreds of children. The result is that there are 650 fewer adoptable children in Colorado in 2020 than there were in 2005.

Mercy tends to deal with the symptoms of a person's life. Empowerment deals with the underlying causes of those symptoms, and we are called to work on both. Jesus said, "Make a tree good and its fruit will be good, or make a tree bad and its fruit will be bad, for a tree is recognized by its fruit" (Matt 12:33). If you want to change the fruit, you've got to change the tree. Mercy is giving people a fish so they are fed for the day. Empowerment is teaching people how to fish, how to own the pond, and even how to zone the pond for fishing.

Believers can make a powerful difference in the lives of others, but it may take a different kind of thinking regarding the best way to help. Robert Lupton writes:

> Ancient Hebrew wisdom describes four levels of charity. At the highest level, the giver provides a job for a person in need without that person knowing who provided it. At the next level, the giver provides work that the needy person knows the giver provided. The third level is an anonymous gift. At the lowest level of charity, which should be avoided whenever possible, the giver gives a gift to a poor person who has full knowledge of the donor's identity. The deepest poverty is to have nothing of value to offer. Charity that fosters such poverty must be challenged. We know that work produces dignity while welfare depletes self-esteem. We know that reciprocity builds mutual respect while one-way giving brews contempt. Yet we continue to run clothes closets and free food pantries and give away benevolence funds, and we wonder why the joy is missing.[2]

Ministries of mercy and empowerment reflect the value of physical well-being. It can be argued that the soul will outlive the body, but both the well-being of the body and that of the soul are equally important to God—and should be to us.

Sometimes people ask, "But what if the people we serve don't respond the way we'd like them to?" The truth is that many people won't come to faith regardless of what evidence they have (Matt 11:20). So, in Luke 17:11–17, we read of Jesus and ten lepers. Lepers were the outcasts of society. Jesus did what only he could do: he cleansed all ten of the lepers. Interestingly, only one in ten returned to Jesus and made the God connection by giving praise to God. We think Jesus knew all along that only one would make the God connection, and yet knowing that nine would go on their merry way didn't prevent him from healing them. He healed them not because they would convert but because they were broken. Likewise, although we believe there is no more fertile ground for evangelism than selfless service, we serve not to convert but because we have been converted. We serve not to make others Christian but because we are Christians. People are worthy recipients whether they become Christ-followers or not. Evangelism is our *ultimate* motive, but it can never be our *ulterior* motive for serving.

John Stott shares his insight regarding motives in service:

> To sum up, we are sent into the world, like Jesus, to serve. For this is the natural expression of our love for our neighbors. We love. We go. We serve. And in this we have (or should have) no ulterior motive. True, the gospel lacks visibility if we merely preach it, and lacks credibility if we who preach it are interested only in souls and have no concern about the welfare of people's bodies, situations and communities. Yet the reason for our acceptance of social responsibility is not primarily in order to give the gospel either a visibility or a credibility it would otherwise lack, but rather simple uncomplicated compassion. Love has no need to justify itself. It merely expresses itself in service wherever it sees need.[3]

## Ministry of Evangelism

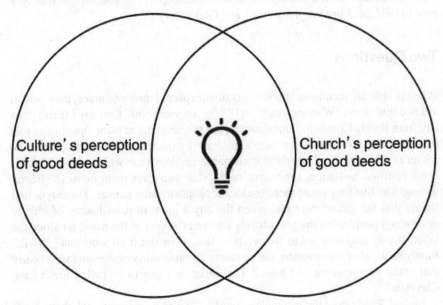

Figure 8.1

Figure 8.1 depicts realms where a church and the surrounding culture might engage in good deeds, as well as the realm of overlap between the two. It is within this space of mutually perceived good where the light shines in such a way that conversations can move toward God. Dave Gibbons, of New Song Church in Santa Ana, California, says, "Justice, advocacy and compassion have to lead the conversation, or it won't be authentic to the next generation."[4] Cru's Ben Ecklu, from a predominantly Muslim country in Africa, says, "In our country, if you come and tell about Christ, you are stoned. If you come to dig a well, the government gives you the land to build a church and protects you from others, and if someone tries to attack you, the government steps in and says, 'No, these are good people.'"[5]

A while back, on a shuttle bus to the airport, I (Eric) sat next to the principal of one of the elementary schools where my church, Calvary Bible Church, did a school makeover through our Sharefest event. When I asked if she had been involved in Sharefest, she replied:

> It brought tears to my eyes to see hundreds of people showing up and working at our school. A youth pastor met with us a few weeks before and asked me, "What is it that you need? What do you want done? Go ahead and dream. I can't guarantee we can do it, but we'll try." Being from Hawaii, I have always wanted an outdoor classroom where teachers could take their students and sit under a tree. And you know what? They did it! By eleven o'clock on Sunday morning, the outdoor classroom was built. The church was amazing!

Good deeds had created goodwill, and in this atmosphere of goodwill, it was very easy to talk about her story, my story, and God's story.

## Two Questions

When people are recipients or observers of unexpected mercy or grace, they tend to ask two questions: "Who are you?" and "Why are you here?" One day I (Eric) got a call from Randy Chestnut. Randy had moved to Cleveland to plant churches as part of a city-wide initiative. Over the phone, Randy explained that he had gone to the mayor of Cleveland and asked the Jesus question: "What can we do for you?" After some justified hesitation, the mayor said, "Can you guys paint houses?" Randy assured him that they could mobilize lots of people to paint houses. The mayor told Randy that the government had given the city a grant to paint houses of elderly or disabled people, but the grant barely covered the cost of the paint, let alone the labor. Randy told him not to worry about that. How did it all work out? "Well," Randy said, "after four months, we've painted around thirty houses and seen nearly that many people come to Christ." The initiative came to be called Fresh Coat Cleveland.[6]

I asked Randy how the evangelism works. "We're very intentional about evangelism," he explained, "since we believe that we're never more like Jesus than when we are serving. So, we expect God to show up in unusual ways. So sometimes the people who live in the house come to Christ. We have people prayer-walking through the neighborhood, and sometimes the people they talk to and pray with come to know Jesus. The last person who came to Christ was a man who lived next door who had to figure out why a dozen people would take a week of vacation to paint a house for a person they didn't even know." Randy's team went on to start a Bible study in that man's home and hoped to turn it into a church plant.

In Omaha, Christ Community Church partnered with public schools and others to help pack and ship 300,000 food packets through the Meals for Mali program. After working side by side with church people, one public-school teacher commented, "I want to be part of a church that is making this type of difference in the world."[7]

## Driving or Putting?

In *Irresistible Evangelism*, Doug Pollock and his co-authors employ the metaphor of golf to help us think clearly about evangelism.[8] He notes that the most highly used evangelistic tools, such as The Four Spiritual Laws, The Bridge, and the Roman Road, were designed when many (if not most) people in our culture shared a common worldview and intellectually knew a lot of the Bible story. They were on the green, very near the hole, and just needed to know how they could take the next step and become a Christian. What the evangelist needed was an evangelistic putter to help with the decision.

Today, only 16 percent of non-Christians ages sixteen to twenty-nine are favorably disposed toward Christianity, with a mere 3 percent favorably disposed toward evangelicals.[9] This means that today people are farther from the green and we need more than one golf club to be effective. What is important is that everything we do moves them closer to the pin. Doug points out that one of the greatest golfers of all time, Tiger Woods, who has been golfing since the age of six, had scored only twenty holes-in-one as of 2019! Even the best golfers take more than one shot to put the ball in the hole. Evangelistic hole-in-one stories are the exception, not the norm. We need to add more clubs to our bag if we want to effectively play today's golf course. Unexpected mercy, grace, or service is a great tee shot that puts the conversation on the fairway.

Doug contrasts approaches that are less and more effective:

| Less Effective | More Effective |
|---|---|
| Telling / Monologue | Listening / Dialogue |
| Compelling proof | Compelling stories |
| Seeking to be understood | Seeking to understand |
| Our language | Their language |
| Rightness / Certainty | Kindness / Mystery |

| | |
|---|---|
| Sharing my God story | Hearing their life story |
| Believing to belong | Belonging before believing |
| Agenda-driven / Scripted | Context-driven / Natural |
| Answers / Winning | Questions / Nudging |
| Gospel presentations | Spiritual conversations[10] |

We really like the approach Doug is taking. (You can find out more about his ministry at GodsGPS.com.)

## Good Deeds and Goodwill

If you study the ministry of Jesus, you will note that almost invariably his good deeds created goodwill among the people around him. After observing the kindness, mercy, and love of Jesus, the Gospels tell us, people in the crowd were in *awe* or *wondered* or were *astonished* or *marveled* or *held Jesus in high esteem.* Good deeds almost always create goodwill with others. Deeds get people's attention more than words can. Nevertheless, goodwill alone does not lead people to faith in Christ, so it is important that we not mistake goodwill for good news.

People on their own often come to erroneous conclusions by just observing the work of God. When the Holy Spirit came upon the believers in Acts 2, the writer records that the onlookers were "amazed and perplexed" and "asked one another, 'What does this mean?'" Others concluded that "they have had too much wine" (Acts 2:12–13). They needed the words of God to explain the work of God, so Peter stood up and began his explanation: "Let me explain this to you; listen carefully to what I say" (Acts 2:14). The result was three thousand people putting their faith in Jesus. In Acts 3, when God healed the beggar through Peter and John, the crowd was "filled with wonder and amazement at what happened to him" (Acts 3:10). Peter again had to give them understanding: "Why does this surprise you? Why do you stare at us as if by our own power or godliness we had made this man walk?" (Acts 3:12). In Act 14 Paul and Barnabas bring healing to a lame man. Immediately the bystanders proclaim, "The gods have come down to us in human form!" and start preparing a sacrifice to them (Acts 14:11–13). Again, words are used—by Paul this time—to explain the meaning of the deeds and to bring them the "good news." Scriptural example after example leads us to believe that God will tee up the conversation through the good deeds, but there is still good news to be shared. We must keep in mind that "faith comes from hearing the message, and the message is heard through the word about Christ" (Rom 10:17). Good deeds may *verify* the good news, but we need good news to *clarify* the meaning of the good deeds.

# WOW!

Water of Life Community Church in Fontana, California, is living out its slogan "Passion for God, Compassion for People." For the past few years, the church has hosted WOW JAM (wowjam.com), a neighborhood festival designed to create community and make Jesus visible in the toughest of communities. At the 2008 WOW JAM, more than four thousand neighbors showed up to eat hamburgers, slurp snow cones, and listen to great local bands. Church people repaired bikes and cooked up 4,100 hamburgers. Pastor Danny Carroll called it "an amazing day" as the good deeds created enough goodwill to create space for over six hundred people to commit their lives to Christ, with eighty of those being baptized over the weekend of WOW JAM. WOW JAM has expanded to seventy-nine cities in thirteen countries and has seen nearly a half million people make decisions for Christ.

Pastor Hal Seed of New Song Community Church sees hundreds of people come to faith every year. Being so close to the US Marine Corps's Camp Pendleton allows the church to be actively engaged in ministering to military families—especially those whose loved ones are deployed. The people of New Song are very committed to both showing their love and telling of God's love. Hal says:

> Events like Operation Yellow Ribbon ("welcome home" parties for returning soldiers) are almost always pre-evangelism events. People can smell inauthenticity a mile away. So, if we hold an event to bless a certain people group, and then we program ten or fifteen minutes in for a gospel presentation, they see it as a bait-and-switch and it actually serves as a negative gospel influence for most attendees. The purpose of a special event like Operation Yellow Ribbon is to extend love, in hopes that the recipients will want to join us. Once they join us, we help them experience the love of Christ and then respond to it. John's gospel tells us that Jesus was full of grace and truth. Most people need grace before they buy our truth. Most churches only offer truth, no grace. That's why we are so intrigued with the externally focused concept. It offers grace. It's about showing and telling.[11]

## The Role of Apologetics

Today we no longer have the home-field advantage. In most social situations, we are the visiting team, so we need to rethink what compelling evidence looks like for those outside the faith. Of course, apologetics (a defense for the reasonableness of Christianity) is still needed today, but most likely the best apologetics will be demonstrated as much as postulated. We think that in many circles, good apologetics is a combination of healthy agnosticism coupled with absolute certainty. What do we mean by that?

So many times, we as Christians feel that to be credible, we have to have all the answers; after all, we do have the truth, don't we? Embracing healthy agnosticism means that we have the freedom to say, "I don't know." So how do we couple agnosticism with certainty? In response to a question about why God would allow or cause an earthquake, tsunami, or other tragedy that takes or breaks innocent lives, we could say, "I could give you some philosophical or religious answers, but I really don't know for certain. But I do know with absolute certainty how Jesus would respond to such a tragedy because there are four books of the New Testament that describe how he did respond to pain and loss and suffering, and that's what my family, friends, and church are trying to do in this situation—to be the hands, feet, and voice of Jesus to those who are hurting."

## Keep It Real

For younger believers, authenticity trumps certainty in apologetics. David Kinnaman, president of the Barna Group and co-author of *UnChristian*, said, "For your generation, your verse was John 3:16; for our generation, it is John 3:17: 'For God sent his Son into the world not to condemn the world but that the world through him might be saved.'" Matt Wilson, director of the Message Trust in Manchester, England, said something similar regarding Christ-followers in England: "For you, it is John 3:16; for us, it is John 3:16–18: 'This is how we know what love is: Jesus Christ laid down his life for us. And we ought to lay down our lives for our brothers. If anyone has material possessions and sees his brother in need but has no pity on him, how can the love of God be in him? Dear children, let us not love with words or tongue but with actions and in truth.'" It seems that most people would still rather *see* a sermon than *hear* a sermon most days of the week.

## Bright Spots in Evangelism

There are some new frontiers where people are regularly coming to faith. We encourage you to investigate how these may raise the evangelistic temperature of your church.

### Neighboring

"What if we began doing the thing that Jesus said matters the most?" That's the question our friend Brian Mavis and I (Rick) asked in our book, *The Neighboring Church: Getting Better at What Jesus Said Matters Most.*[12] Are we loving God and loving our neighbors as ourselves? Brian likes to say, "Just taking that small step to know our neighbors' names is like taking a small step on a moving sidewalk— and the magic begins." The watchword question a generation ago was "If your church were to disappear, would the community notice and would the community care?" Today that question takes a more granular form: "If you were to leave your neighborhood, would anyone notice and would anyone care?"

Our good friends Dave Runyon and Jay Pathak have created a refrigerator magnet that sits on the doors of over 400,000 refrigerators around the country. The yellow magnet has nine boxes representing your neighborhood, and the first step to good neighboring is simply to know the names of the eight neighbors around you. Neighboring is not a "so that" evangelistic strategy—"I'll be a good neighbor *so that* I can share the gospel." Be a good neighbor because that's what Jesus wants us to do and then . . . "let the magic begin."

## Alpha

Alpha is a series of interactive sessions that explore Christianity. Birthed out of Holy Trinity Brompton Church in the United Kingdom, Alpha now runs courses around the globe. In Canada over one million people (one out of every thirty Canadians) has been through an Alpha course. An Alpha course typically takes place over eleven weeks, ending with a retreat. Alpha runs in cafés, university campuses, businesses, and churches. Each session begins with food served—ranging from coffee and cake to a full meal. This is followed by a short talk (usually on video) on some aspect of Christianity contextualized to the country and language. Then comes the best part: the chance to share thoughts and ideas on the topic. Everyone is encouraged to share their thoughts and perspective in an open, friendly, and accepting environment. And there are no "wrong" answers. Alpha is super effective because it is in sync with the way people investigate God today on their journey to faith. A 2019 Barna study disclosed that the top qualities nonbelievers look for in a person with whom they could talk about faith are:

- "Listens without judgment" (62 percent)
- "Does not force a conclusion" (50 percent)
- "Allows others to draw their own conclusions" (49 percent)
- "Demonstrates interest in other people's story or life" (29 percent)[13]

Barna's findings are not unlike what others are discovering about how people move in their faith journey. In 2008 after interviewing thousands of people who came to faith as adults, two InterVarsity staff members, Don Everts and Doug Schaupp, discovered that each had crossed five thresholds in their journey to faith:

1. From distrusting a Christian to TRUSTING a Christian
2. From indifference to being CURIOUS
3. From being closed to change to being OPEN TO CHANGE
4. From being open to change to SEEKING AFTER JESUS
5. From seeking after Jesus to FOLLOWING JESUS

The Alpha course follows this same pattern toward becoming a Christ-follower. You can dive deeper into Everts and Schaupp's journey in their book, *I Once Was Lost: What Postmodern Skeptics Taught Us about Their Path to Jesus.*[14]

## Externally Focused Ministry

In 2015 I (Eric) surveyed twenty-nine churches I had helped to establish their externally focused ministries. These were large churches averaging over three thousand in weekend attendance. Together they had seen over nine thousand people come to faith in 2014, which averaged one new Christian for every ten attendees. Eighty-three percent of these churches experienced numerical growth in 2014. Here are a few interesting results from the survey:

- "Serving others selflessly as a church, with no expectations of anything in return, helps create a plausibility structure for the truth of the gospel." – 83% strongly agreed; 17% somewhat agreed

- "I find it easier and more likely to have spiritual conversations with nonbelievers because of the good our church is doing in the community." – 51% strongly agreed; 40% somewhat agreed

- "Nonbelievers are coming to faith because of the good we are doing in the community." – 36% strongly agreed; 55% somewhat agreed

- "We are more effective evangelistically because we engage in serving our community outside the walls of our church." – 62% strongly agreed; 34% somewhat agreed

- "Nonbelievers are becoming part of our church because of the good we are doing in the community." – 26% strongly agreed; 70% somewhat agreed

- "Our community is healthier and better off because our church is active in the community." – 91% strongly agreed; 8% somewhat agreed

- "To have a voice or presence in our community we must be engaged in meeting the needs of our community . . . not just having great church events." – 94% strongly agreed; 6% somewhat agreed

## Increasing Spiritual Conversations through Service

Sometimes when we serve, we do so in the context of an all-church weekend event, like a Sharefest or Serve Day, and we are not serving beside nonbelievers. We can still create hundreds of evangelistic conversations simply by saying, "This week tell five people, 'I had a great weekend,' and then just shut up. If God is in the conversation, people will respond with curiosity and questions and say something like, 'What did you do?' You can then tell them, 'I served alongside three hundred other Christ-followers painting, washing windows, and landscaping the local elementary school. We're just trying to figure out what Jesus would do if he were walking among us and then do that. And we do a lot of other things like that to serve our community.' Let God take it from there!" If three hundred people had five spiritual conversations that week, that would be fifteen hundred conversations that might otherwise never have taken place.

Being the best church *for* the community may very well be the best way to see people come to faith and become part of a community that is changing the world.

## What Can We Learn about Evangelism from "Evangelists"?

Guy Kawasaki is recognized as one of the leading thinkers in marketing. He's also a committed Christ-follower. In a blog post, Kawasaki notes that out of curiosity, he searched a job-posting site for jobs using the key word *evangelist*. He reports, "Amazingly, there were 611 matches—and none were for churches. It seems that 'evangelist' is now a secular, mainstream job title." Reading through the different job descriptions, he sums up the ten "fundamental principles of evangelism":

1. *Create a cause.* . . . The starting point of evangelism is having a great thing to evangelize. A cause seizes the moral high ground. It is a product or service that improves the lives of people, ends bad things, or perpetuates good things. . . .

2. *Love the cause.* "Evangelist" isn't simply a job title. It's a way of life. It means that the evangelist totally loves the product and sees it as a way to bring the "good news." A love of the cause is the second most important determinant of the success of an evangelist—second only to the quality of the cause itself. No matter how great the person, if he doesn't love the cause, he cannot be a good evangelist for it.

3. *Look for agnostics, ignore atheists.* A good evangelist can usually tell if people understand and like a product in five minutes. If they don't, cut your losses and avoid them. It is very hard to convert someone to a new religion (i.e., product) when he believes in another god (i.e., another product). . . .

4. *Localize the pain.* No matter how revolutionary your product, don't describe it using lofty, flowery terms like "revolutionary," "paradigm shifting," and "curve jumping." . . . People don't buy "revolutions." They buy "aspirins" to fix the pain or "vitamins" to supplement their lives.

5. *Let people test drive the cause.* Essentially, say to people, "We think you are smart. Therefore, we aren't going to bludgeon you into becoming our customer. Try our product, take it home, download it, and then decide if it's right for you." . . .

6. *Learn to give a demo.* An "evangelist who cannot give a great demo" is an oxymoron. A person simply cannot be an evangelist if she cannot demo the product. . . .

7. *Provide a safe first step.* The path to adopting a cause should have a slippery slope. . . . For example, the safe first step to recruit an evangelist for the environment is not requiring that she chain herself to a tree; it's to ask her to start recycling and taking shorter showers.

8. *Ignore pedigrees.* Good evangelists aren't proud. They don't focus on the people with big titles and big reputations. Frankly, they'll meet with, and

help, anyone who "gets it." . . .

9. *Never tell a lie.* Very simply, lying is morally and ethically wrong. . . . If one always tells the truth, then there's nothing to keep track of. Evangelists know their stuff, so they never have to tell a lie to cover their ignorance.

10. *Remember your friends.* Be nice to the people on the way up because one is likely to see them again on the way down. Once an evangelist has achieved success, he shouldn't think that he'll never need those folks again. . . .[15]

We think Kawasaki's insights are particularly valuable and fit completely with how evangelism works today.

## The Leadership Challenge

As a leader, you can really help people move along the continuum from good deeds to good will to good news. In evangelism, teach your people to recognize the "God moment"—the time that God enters a conversation. God moments are characterized by curiosity and questions. When a person asks questions like "Who are you?" and "Why are you doing this?" you can be certain that God has entered that conversation.

# 9.

# Creativity: They Innovate, Not Replicate

*The real acts of discovery consist not in finding new lands but in seeing with new eyes.*

—Attributed to Marcel Proust

In 2009, Leadership Network, in partnership with the Hartford Institute for Religion Research, conducted a study to find out how large churches that describe themselves as "innovative" differ from other churches. The results were both revealing and enlightening. Highly innovative churches

- grow faster than other churches;

- have a higher rate of new believers than other churches;

- put more emphasis on personal Bible study and tithing than other churches;

- experience less conflict than other churches.

Ninety-one percent of the people attending highly innovative churches strongly agree that their church "has a clear mission and purpose" and see themselves as "a positive force for good in [their] community." These innovative churches have more volunteers and are significantly more likely to invite friends and family to church. The author of the survey, Warren Bird, makes some insightful observations: "Churches that welcome innovation tend to embrace creativity, ingenuity, and divergent ways of thinking *inside* the box. They have a willingness to change their practice in order to improve performance. Their bent is to solve problems [in ways] that will generate better results—such as more and better disciples of Jesus Christ."[1]

Warren's insights are important. Churches don't innovate simply to be novel, cute, or clever; they innovate to achieve their God-given mission.

## Ideation, Creativity, Inspiration, Invention—and Innovation

We want first of all to clarify what innovation is *not* on the way to discovering what it is. Innovation is *not* the same as ideation, creativity, inspiration, or invention. To be certain, creativity, inspiration, and ideation are important to the innovative process, but innovation always pertains to the *productive application* of creativity. Tom Kelley of the global design company Ideo reminds us that "all good working definitions of innovation pair ideas with action, the spark with the fire." Drilling down further, he quotes the 3M company's definition of innovation: "new ideas—plus action or implementation—which result in an improvement, a gain, or a profit."[2] Thomas Edison is said to have pointed out that "an idea is called an invention. Converting an idea into something that is useful to the customer and profitable for the company is called innovation."[3] Elaine Dundon defines *innovation* as "the profitable implementation of strategic creativity."[4] It is innovation that brings ideas to life.

Innovation deals with being not simply novel or different but "better." And it is important to think about where we put our innovative energies and to not mistake innovation for uniqueness, creativity, or cleverness. Innovation needs to be tied to results that matter in regard to your mission. So, having a children's area that looks like Disneyland may be creative, but it may not be innovative. Having candles in the back of the church may be creative but not necessarily innovative. Writing your own follow-up or discipleship materials may be creative but not necessarily innovative—if they do not change the outcomes compared to using materials that already exist. In areas that are not mission-critical, we can replicate what has been done. Creative and innovative energy should be reserved for the growth plates that are crucial to accomplishing your mission.

## Results and Effort

Innovation always pertains to the relationship between inputs and outcomes—between effort and resources expended on the one hand, and the result or fruit of the outcome on the other. Look at the diagram in figure 9.1. Many churches are in the upper-left quadrant—they are getting results according to their effort. Their budgets, programs, and staff are accomplishing what they were intended to accomplish. In the lower-left quadrant are churches that spend much but accomplish little toward their mission. In the lower-right quadrant are churches that expend little and accomplish little. They are simply in survival mode.

To be honest, all of us would like to be in the upper-right quadrant: accomplishing more while using fewer resources and expending less effort to do so. To do so requires innovation. The upper right quadrant is where we find people like Gideon's three hundred men and the boy with five loaves of bread and two fish.

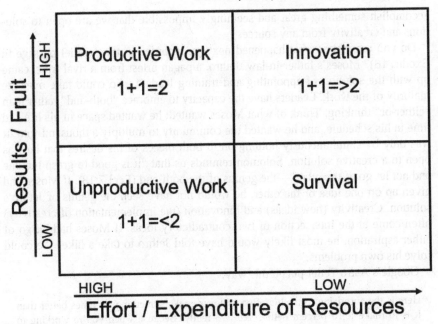

Figure 9.1

## The One Condition for Innovation

Anyone whose goals are bigger than their resources can be an innovator. If you are content with the status quo, there is no need to innovate. Innovation thrives under the conditions of scarcity or opportunity, but it never happens unless the leader has a goal. Genuine innovation occurs not because a person is trying to be original but because a person is attempting something difficult.

Let's take a look at Moses in Deuteronomy 1. Deuteronomy is the record of three speeches given by Moses to prepare the Israelites to enter the promised land. In his first address, he said to the Israelites, "At that time I said to you, 'You are too heavy a burden for me to carry alone. The Lord your God has increased your numbers so that today you are as many as the stars in the sky. May the Lord, the God of your fathers, *increase you a thousand times* and bless you as he has promised!'" (Deut 1:9–11).

You have just read about the heart of a leader. "You are way more than I can handle. I don't think I can do this job one more day, but my prayer is that God would multiply you *a thousand times more!*" As burned-out as Moses was, he still wanted God to do a thousand times more. He didn't shrink the size of his vision to the size of his capacity. Leaders have a way to hold two seemingly contrary things in their mind until they discover the solution. Moses didn't succumb to "either-or" thinking. He wanted more time in his schedule and space in his life, *and* he wanted to see God multiply the Israelites by a thousand times. It is only when we want to accomplish something great and seemingly impossible that we are open to solutions and creativity from any source.

Do you remember what happened next (as recorded in the parallel passage in Exodus 18)? Moses's father-in-law, Jethro, a pagan priest from a rival tribe, came up with the solution of appointing and training leaders who could take over the majority of the work. Leaders have the capacity to embrace "both-and" rather than "either-or" thinking. Think of what Moses wanted: he wanted space in his life and time in his schedule, and he wanted the community to multiply a thousand-fold. It was only by simultaneously holding on to both pieces of his desires that he was open to a creative solution. Solomon reminds us that "it is good to grasp the one and not let go of the other"—the genius of the both-and (Eccl 7:18). If Moses had given up on one idea or the other, he would not have seen the genius of Jethro's solution. Creativity (new ideas) and innovation (the implementation of creativity) often come at the intersection of two contradictory ideas. If Moses had let go of either aspiration, he most likely would have told Jethro to take a hike—he could solve his own problems.

Google's Astro Teller puts it this way:

> Here is the surprising truth: It's often easier to make something 10 times better than it is to make it 10 percent better. Yes . . . really. Because when you're working to make things 10 percent better, you inevitably focus on the existing tools and assumptions, and on building on top of an existing solution that many people have already spent a lot of time thinking about. Such incremental progress is driven by extra effort, extra money, and extra resources. It's tempting to feel improving things this way means we're being good soldiers, with the grit and perseverance to continue where others may have failed—but most of the time we find ourselves stuck in the same old slog. But when you aim for a 10x gain, you lean instead on bravery and creativity—the kind that, literally and metaphorically, can put a man on the moon.[5]

## Feeding the Fifty Thousand (Every Day)

A few summers ago, I (Eric) flew to southern California to be part of Serve Day, a one-day service project involving dozens of churches and more than five thousand volunteers. Serve Day was begun as a one-time initiative by Rock Harbor Church in Costa Mesa, California, as an alternative to worship because their usual meeting place had been double-booked one week. *Serving* on Sunday was an innovative alternative to Sunday *service*. But the event had multiplied over the years.

After Serve Day, my good friend Eric Marsh took me around to see some of the externally focused initiatives in the Long Beach area. One of the most amazing people I met was Arlene Mercer, founder of Food Finders in Long Beach (foodfinders.org). In 1989, Arlene became aware of all the hungry people in this community near Los Angeles. But what could she do by herself? She had no warehouse in which to store or distribute food. But what she did have was an innovative idea. What if she could connect the restaurants and grocery stores that threw out clean, edible food every day with agencies that fed hungry people? "What could be" was converted to "what is." From its beginnings years ago in Arlene's thrift store, Food Finders has come a long way: it now works with 230 human-service organizations and, following her innovative storefront model, feeds some 50,000 children and sick, elderly, and homeless people in Orange County and Los Angeles every day! Over the past thirty years, Food Finders has been responsible for distributing over 125 million meals' worth of food—without ever having to store one item. Arlene's probably a person you have never heard of, but she is cutting a huge swath for the kingdom.

## What Do You Want to Accomplish?

So, what do you want to accomplish that is so big that currently, you don't have the resources to accomplish it? Leaders always have the ability to create something that doesn't currently exist with resources they don't currently have. What keeps you awake at night? What do you find yourself thinking about? Where do your thoughts gravitate? What peppers your conversation with other kingdom-minded believers? How do you want to change the world? What evil should die in your community because your church exists? What good should thrive? How will people, communities, relationships, and cities be different if God grants you the desire of your heart? Having a compelling dream pulls you forward; it allows you to say yes to people and opportunities to get where you want to go (think of Nehemiah before the king), and to say no to things that would derail your mission (think of Joseph before Potiphar's wife). A big, compelling dream is the criterion by which you measure opportunities for innovation. If entrepreneurship involves shifting resources from lower to higher value, what is it that you really value? Rich Nathan, senior pastor of the Vineyard Church in Columbus, Ohio, expresses his dream:

> We need a larger target than simply building a great church. We want to live in a great city. We don't want the church to simply be an oasis in a great desert. We would like to live in a city where people are not shredded as they go to work in their companies because the moral environment of their companies is so dehumanizing. When people walk out the doors of this church, we don't want to send them back to places in our city that are plagued by gangs. We don't want to send our kids back to schools where they have to be afraid of being attacked or where very little learning actually takes place. We want to send people of this church out into a city that has access to medical care, where there is an availability of jobs, where the races are getting along and there is racial understanding.[6]

How can we make the shift from trying to be the best church *in* the community to being the best church *for* the community?

## Shifting Resources

When you make the switch from wanting to be the best church *in* the community to being the best church *for* the community, you have made a shift of tectonic proportions in moving all of your resources from a lower to a higher value and to a greater yield. Within your church, you have the same resources at your disposal to become the best church *for* the community as you have for being the best church *in* the community. The difference is whether you will use them to focus inward or to focus outward. What resources are we talking about?

As we mentioned in chapter 4, Reggie McNeal and I (Eric) gave leadership to a Leadership Network cohort called Missional Renaissance Leadership Community. The idea comes from the cross-pollination of ideas that began in fifteenth-century Florence, Italy, resulting in the Renaissance. Reggie and I brought together cross-domain leaders from church, government, business, and human services to work toward the missional transformation of their cities. These leadership communities met four times over a two-year period. Each gathering began with a report of what they had accomplished in the previous six months, along with what they learned along the way, and ended with a six-moth plan toward their epic win.

Making the shift from an internal to an external focus involves shifting the value of the resources at hand. What resources are available to us, and how can we raise their value? Reggie helps us see that all churches have the exact same resources at their disposal: people, facilities, prayer, finances, technology, and time. How these resources are expended is what makes the difference.

## People (Leaders and Others)

People are a church's most important resource, yet most churches view people as consumers of religious goods and services and the church as the vendor of those same religious goods and services. How can we raise the value of the contribution of people? Let's start with leaders. The contribution of leaders is enhanced as they take on the responsibility to equip the saints for service (Eph 4:11) and help people discover and live out their Ephesians 2:10 calling. They ask people, "What do you love to do? How can God use that for ministry?"

Here's the point: the contribution of people greatly increases when they move from Ephesians 2:8–9 to Ephesians 2:10, from coming to Jesus to hear his words and be healed of their diseases, to serving and giving; from being spectators and consumers of religious goods and services, to being contributors and producers of spiritual life and vitality. God puts leaders in the church to help everyone in the church live "on mission," and that process comes through "people development."

When Christ-followers are living on mission, they become kingdom people, and kingdom people think about the spiritual, relational, and physical well-being of others. In an externally focused church, every person is on mission. The value of the contribution of people is exponentially raised as they serve outside the walls of the church. How do leaders get people serving in the community? Lead Pastor Mike Kessler of Trinity Church in Mount Pleasant, Texas, says, "We have basically adopted the city calendar, and we've provided volunteers for just about every event that the community has had." It is *people* that cause a church to be the best church *for* the community.

Over the years, we have both had the opportunity to meet a lot of high-capacity people, and one consistent scenario is how underutilized they are in their local churches. In fact, many of them join boards of national or international ministries or get engaged in some of the larger nonprofit groups in their community. They are looking for something big to do, and they don't see the church as a place in which to devote their entrepreneurial energies toward innovation.

A few years ago, I (Rick) pulled together a group of successful businesspeople; most own or owned their companies. A few are now retired, but most are still very active in their businesses. They have one common characteristic: they get things done—and usually get them done in a big way. They are high-capacity people. Here was my attempt at giving them a million-dollar idea: "I'd like to start a behind-the-scenes group of high-capacity people to do a couple of things. First, I want this group to spend part of its time looking at how God can use us to make a difference in the world. Second, I'd like to invite some of our community leaders in to discuss the big issues they see in our community and for us to tackle one. Third, I have no idea how we will move things forward." Out of several conversations like that, the Dulos group formed. (*Dulos* is the Greek word for "servant.")

At first, about a dozen people were involved; eventually, it grew closer to twenty. We listened to leaders tell about the significant issues in the community; the group settled on the struggles of single mothers. The formation of Dulos marked not only the expansion of that area of ministry for LifeBridge, but also the beginning of LifeBridge's transition from focus on mercy to focus on justice.

Here is what the high-capacity folks in churches, government agencies, and nonprofits can do that most of us don't do so well: they generally think in terms of sustainable solutions, moving forward, and leveraging opportunities. They are the people who often think up million-dollar ideas or give wings to them. They know that with greater risk can come greater rewards. These five-talent people (Matt 25:15) are looking for a way to use their gifts, talents, and experience to be a part of what God is up to. How are we helping them do that? How might high-capacity people change what we measure as we seek to be the best church *for* the community? Listed below are a few of the changes deemed necessary by leaders who have been trying to make the shift from an internal to an external focus.

| Internal Focus | External Focus |
| --- | --- |
| Church people | Kingdom people |
| Clergy and laity | Everyone on mission |
| Number of people who attend | Number of people who are released to serve, start, or lead ministries |
| "What do we need?" | "What does the community need?" |
| Small groups and Sunday school "for us" | Mentoring and tutoring "for them" |
| People consuming religious goods and services | People equipped to serve others |

| | |
|---|---|
| Trying to bring in more people "like us" | Trying to serve others unlike us |
| Loving what we do | Loving people and what they do |
| Growing people through church | Growing people through service programs |
| People in the pews | People in the streets |
| People in programs | People development |
| "How's our church doing?" | "How's our city doing?" |

## Facilities

How can you raise the value of your facilities from a lower to a greater societal impact? Most church facilities sit empty much of the week. What would it be like to open your facilities to other community organizations? That's what externally focused churches do to extract the maximum value from their facilities.

When music legend Isaac Hayes died in August 2009 and his family was looking for a place to host a memorial tribute, they approached the leaders of Hope Church in the Memphis area. Craig Strickland, Hope's senior pastor at the time, readily agreed to host the event in the church's 5,000-seat auditorium—whereupon placard-filled protests and outcries ensued on the part of many in the local conservative Christian community because Hayes was a Scientologist.

Nevertheless, the leaders at Hope held their ground. "We're trying to do something good for the community to bring it together," Craig told the media. "That's what the church is for."[7] Clearly, Hope Church has a firm vision of being the best church *for* the community. Its director of missions, Eli Morris, added, "Hayes lived in our neighborhood, and his baby child is in our preschool. This is something we sensed God wanted us to do."[8] Interestingly, as the result of the Isaac Hayes tribute, many people who attended the service have come back to Hope to get closer to God. This approach is not new to Hope, which often makes its facilities available for private and public school events such as graduations and celebrations.

Several years ago, when the Vineyard Church of Columbus was engaged in a building campaign to expand its facility, it dedicated 50,000 square feet to a community center that houses medical and dental offices, a gymnasium, a kids' play area, a dance and aerobics studio, and space for after-school tutoring for immigrant children and their parents.

One of the biggest needs of every community is people to help elementary school students with reading, as learning to read by the third grade is the most predictive factor regarding a child's future. But who has time during the week to visit a local school? Would it be possible to create a win-win situation by providing two to three hours of free childcare each week at the church to every parent who volunteers an hour a week at the school? Parents could help the kids at school and have a little downtime for themselves before returning to pick up their own kids at church. What parent wouldn't love that?

When founding pastor John Bruce of Creekside Community Church in San Leandro, California, wanted to purchase a former restaurant for his thriving church plant, the city told him that the community already had enough churches and had in fact denied the requests of nine other would-be buyers and church planters. So, John went back to the drawing board. Remember, innovation happens best when big goals are accompanied by acute shortages. Could the city use a community center that would serve its people? The answer was a hesitant yes, and Creekside was granted a renovation permit. For the past twenty years, the church has opened the facility to schools, community organizations, and the people they serve. In 2019, for example, apart from church programming, the church hosted three Red Cross blood drives; held a Valentine's Day ball for over one hundred developmentally disabled adults; hosted two graduation ceremonies; raised thousands of dollars and deployed forty people to love vulnerable children and their families; hosted a community craft fair that raised $5,000 for the local women's shelter; hosted a day program for the homeless population of San Leandro the first, third, and fifth Sundays of the month, providing showers, haircuts, clothing, social services, and a warm meal to fifty to one hundred people experiencing homelessness each month; and facilitated myriad other externally focused efforts. John has brilliantly figured out how to leverage the value of the Creekside facility and is discovering what it means to be the best church *for* the community.

In 2019, the mayor presented Creekside with the "City Where Kindness Matters" award in recognition of their love for the city. John's insightful lesson after twenty years of community engagement? "Ministries that don't result in relationships are a poor use of our time. We've found that we have to be connected with people socially in order to influence them spiritually; and ministries where we simply parachute in goods and services but are unable to connect with the people who need those goods and services don't last." This church of six hundred may have a smaller shoe size but it has a huge footprint in the community.

In 1872, pioneering church planter Sheldon Jackson established First Presbyterian Church in downtown Boulder, Colorado. First Pres has always been a church for the city, but in 2020 they launched a plan to restructure their buildings to align more closely with their vision. Under the banner "For Boulder with Love," along changing their name to Grace Commons Church, they declared:

> Our buildings will be radically updated and improved with the needs of our neighbors front-of-mind. Open common spaces to gather, dedicated spaces for kids to play, and affordable housing are just a few of the many changes to our facilities that will allow us to more fully live out our vision of love for Boulder.[9]

We believe that church facilities exist for the benefit of the community and that externally focused churches actively look for ways to allow groups to use them. Think about your church. How would you use your facilities if you wanted to be the best church *for* the community? The table below presents the changes in thinking needed to shift from an internal to an external focus.

| Internal Focus | External Focus |
|---|---|
| Facilities are for the church. | Facilities are for church and community. |
| Counting church people here on Sunday. | Counting people who use the facility during the week. |
| We need to protect our facilities. | We need to wear out our facilities. |
| Facilities are designed for the congregation. | Facilities are designed to bless the congregation and community. |
| This is "our church house." | This is "our community house." |
| Keep the facilities for ourselves. | Offer facilities to the community. |

## Prayer

How can you leverage prayer from a lower level to a higher level of impact? When we pray for people outside of our own congregations, we are taking prayer to a new level. A few years ago as the pastors of our community in Boulder, Colorado, were trying to figure out how to serve the city, we concluded that the best way to begin was to ask the leaders who served the city—the mayor, the chief of police, the district attorney, the university president, the superintendent of schools, the city planner, and the city manager, among others. During our monthly luncheons, we asked these city leaders to share a little bit about their responsibilities, their vision of a healthy community, and three impossible things they wanted to accomplish that no person could do for them. This was our way of asking these leaders for prayer requests, since our God is known for operating in the area of impossibilities. Our customary way to end these gatherings was simply to bless and pray for the "impossible" requests of these leaders.

The results were pretty amazing. As we prayed, one leader wiped tears from his eyes and said, "I know people have prayed for me before, but I've never heard anyone pray out loud for me before." Another community leader said, "I came here with apprehension, but I realize I am among friends." Another leader called a couple of months later to ask if she could return and give the pastors three more requests, since all of her "impossibles" had since been answered and resolved. One leader, after being prayed for and blessed, said, "This was one of the greatest days of my life." We often underestimate that fact that everyone wants to be blessed, and it is within the province of Christian leaders to give such blessings.

When Israel was in exile in Babylon and trying to figure out how to follow and serve God in captivity, God sent them this message: "This is what . . . God . . . says to all those I carried into exile from Jerusalem to Babylon: . . . Seek the peace and prosperity of the city to which I have carried you into exile. Pray to the Lord for it, because if it prospers, you too will prosper" (Jer 29:4–7).

The value of prayer is elevated to a new level when we pray for our neighbors, our enemies, and our city. How do we change what we measure on the way to becoming the best church *for* the community? Below are provides some answers.

| Internal Focus | External Focus |
| --- | --- |
| Prayer inside the church | Prayer on location in the community (schools, places of violence, etc.) |
| Prayer for our people | Prayer for those outside our church—city officials, human service agency leaders, teachers, etc. |
| Prayer for our church | Prayer for other churches |
| Prayer *for* you | Prayer *with* you |
| Prayer for church finances | Prayer for money to be freed up to help others |
| Prayer for the lost in our church | Prayer for and engagement with three people who don't know Jesus |
| Prayer gatherings for people in our church | Prayer gatherings with other churches for the community |
| Prayer for myself (my happiness, security, health, etc.) | Prayer for people in need |
| Prayer for God to change "them" | Prayer for God to change me |
| Prayer for people to come to church | Prayer for people to be sent out from our church |
| Prayer for the success of our church | Prayer for expansion of the kingdom |
| People who pray | People of prayer |

## Finances

Few things about the church are as internally focused as our use of finances. Twenty years ago, one study showed that

- 97 percent of total church income in 2000 was spent on costs benefiting Christians;
- 3 percent of total income was spent on costs benefiting non-Christians;

- 106 times more money was spent on the salaries of full-time ministers serving Christians than on the salaries of ministers working with non-Christians; and

- virtually all (99.62 percent) of every dollar is spent to benefit the congregation rather than the community.[10]

Hopefully we've gotten more externally focused since then, but if the resources in the pockets of believers could be shifted from a lower return to a higher return, the impact would be incredible. In 2005 "Christians who attend[ed] church twice a month or more . . . earned a collective income of . . . more than $2 trillion . . . more than the total GDP of every nation in the world except the six wealthiest."[11] Furthermore, if US church members tithed 10 percent of their income each year, they could evangelize the world, stop the daily deaths of 29,000 children younger than five worldwide, provide elementary education across the globe, and tackle domestic poverty—and still have $150 billion left over.[12]

But externally focused churches that want to become the best church *for* their community think and act differently. In 2006, three pastors, Chris Seay, Greg Holder, and Rick McKinley, sensed that they were missing something about Christmas. Where was the connection between the birth of the Savior and our shopping lists? Each Christmas we spend over half a billion dollars on presents but the world is no different afterward. Could Christmas still change the world? They came up with a brilliant idea called the Advent Conspiracy movement, involving four countercultural concepts:

- Worship Fully—because Christmas begins and ends with Jesus.

- Spend Less—and free your resources for things that truly matter.

- Give More—of your presence: your hands, your words, your time, your heart.

- Love All—the poor, the forgotten, the marginalized, and the sick in ways that make a difference.

They talked a few of their church buddies into joining them on this journey, and Advent Conspiracy was born. Over the past fifteen years, thousands of churches in over forty countries have joined the Advent Conspiracy movement. The external impact has been amazing as churches channel more resources to the poor, marginalized, and forgotten. It was estimated that by 2018, Advent Conspiracy churches had raised over $16.2 million for Living Water International—and that's just *one* of countless organizations that have been served! Christmas is still changing the world.

Ohio was hit particularly hard by the 2008 recession. On Palm Sunday in 2009, Pastor Rich Nathan gave the congregants of the Vineyard Church of Columbus the opportunity to help people in the community who were on the verge of losing their homes due to foreclosure. The people of the Vineyard stepped up and gave $625,000 in cash and checks to help keep people in their homes. (The church's former record for a special collection was about $250,000 contributed for Hurricane Katrina relief.)

Medical debt is an odious kind of debt in that it never goes away.[13] In February 2020 Brian Tome, lead pastor of Crossroads Cincinnati church announced that the people of Crossroads were able to pay off $46.5 million in medical bills for 41,233 people in 103 ZIP codes across 3 states. Working with a nonprofit called RIP Medical Debt, Crossroads was able to leverage each dollar they raised over a ten-day period to pay off $100 in medical debt. According to RIP Medical Debt, the "Crossroads' campaign is its largest amount of medical debt that's ever been retired."[14] But this is also a great way for smaller churches to leverage their finances. Although Revolution Church in Annapolis, Maryland, has no permanent building and a weekend attendance of a mere 200, they were able to wipe out $1.9 million in medical debt for 900 families in 2019.[15]

A while back, I (Eric) was in New Zealand talking about externally focused churches to a group of leaders gathered at Spreydon Baptist Church in Christchurch—a church whose DNA winds thick around the poor and marginalized in the local community. The people of Spreydon Baptist are engaged in a number of externally focused efforts and have been for many years. A few years earlier, some folks in the church tried to identify the biggest need of their community. Their answer? Consumer debt. So they started a "bank" in their church called Kingdom Resources (kingdomresources.org.nz). Because debt is eating many people for lunch, Kingdom Resources, after screening and debt counseling, lends the money to debtors to pay off their debt in full, charging them zero interest on their loan.

The concept is based on a few key ideas they linked together. First, many believers have money sitting idle in private banks earning a mere 1 to 2 percent in interest—money that could be used for the kingdom. Many people are trapped in high-interest loans they will never be able to get out from under. The money is pooled from believers who want to put their money to good and godly use. Contributors put in between $100 and $100,000. When Eric was there, Spreydon had already loaned out over $2.6 million to the people of Christchurch and was helping them learn about budgeting, money management, saving programs, and other financial strategies.

Over the years, the payback rate has been 98 percent. Kingdom Resources has also trained 130 "budget counselors" to help folks with budget advice as well as employment, life, and spiritual counseling. They are setting the captives free. It's really about "little people helping little people," says Spreydon's pastor emeritus, Murray Robertson.

How does becoming the best church for the community affect the way we understand and deploy our finances? Here are some answers.

| Internal Focus | External Focus |
| --- | --- |
| How much we keep | How much we give away |
| Church is a holding tank | Church is a pipeline |
| Scarcity mentality | Abundance mentality (loaves and fishes) |
| Church savings | Microloans |
| Giving | Empowering |
| Pledge drives | Jesus-like generosity |
| Paying for things | Providing seed money |
| Giving to the church | Giving to the church and other organizations |

## Technology

Technology provides the enabling mechanisms that we use to be more efficient or effective in accomplishing our mission and vision. One of the best things about technology is that it is "content-neutral," so it can be quickly repurposed from internal use to external use. Externally focused churches use their technology not just to extend their reach but also to extend their blessing. When two dozen other churches in Orange County, California, wanted to join Rock Harbor Church in Costa Mesa for Serve Day, Rock Harbor's technology team built a website that enabled five thousand people to sign up for 275 different projects in the county. When a work project was filled with the required number of volunteers, that project "disappeared" from the site, so it always appeared that every opportunity to serve was still open. Project team leaders had the names and contact information for each of their volunteers. The technology was seamless.

In past generations, the local church was a center for both content and community. If you wanted to receive the content of the message, the spiritual stimulus of worship, and the fellowship with believers, you needed to show up at a certain place at a certain time. It worked—then. But with the advent and proliferation of online content and online community, the need to show up at a certain place at a certain time is disappearing, not just for content but also for community, especially among young people. In 2018 it was reported that the average person in the US sends thirty-two text messages every day.[16] In the past few years, technology has enabled not just the one (the preacher) to broadcast to the many via Facebook Live, webinars, YouTube, or the like, but has evolved so radically that the many can communicate with and contribute to the many—which allows community to form.

The 2020 coronavirus created a tipping point in how churches experimented with and implemented technology. As churches were prohibited from gathering in physical spaces they had to be creative in discovering other ways to connect with the people in the city and connect with and grow the congregants in their church.

Necessity became the midwife to new innovative practices to fulfill their mission. How can you use technology to create community for those outside the walls of your church? How can you use technology to connect people in the church to the needs and dreams outside of the church? This table may give you some ideas.

| **Internal Focus** | **External Focus** |
| --- | --- |
| The church camp | The church mission |
| How to navigate and understand the church | How to navigate and understand the community |
| Videos of church activities | Videos making others the hero |
| Mobilizing the church | Mobilizing the community |
| Creating opportunities to connect to the church | Creating opportunities to connect to the community |
| Equipment under lock and key | Equipment shared with the community |
| Accumulating data | Telling the stories |
| Expert-built content | Community-built content |
| Internal church-based links | Links to other churches and community partners |

## Time

How we spend our time and how we spend our money are probably the two most determinative things about us. Some churches build into the job descriptions of every staff person a half-day of volunteering in a human-service agency in their community. Other churches ask that all staff be involved in one hour of tutoring in the public schools each week. Some churches, such as Perimeter Church in Atlanta, designate full-time and part-time staff to engage, connect, and collaborate in the community. Time invested in the community has economic value estimated at $25.43 per hour as of 2018.[17] Imagine the impact of a church of six hundred giving just two hours per person per week, investing in schools for nine months of the year. The economic value would be $1,098,576. That's a lot of transformational capital!

How is the value of time raised when a church moves from being internally focused to being externally focused?

| Internal Focus | External Focus |
| --- | --- |
| Busyness | Effectiveness |
| Hours spent in church | Hours spent serving others |
| Small groups work for the church | Small groups engage the community |
| Time spent with believers | Time spent with nonbelievers in redemptive relationships |
| Number of children in Sunday school | Number of children reading at grade level |
| Staff clocking in | Staff clocking out |
| Time spent in the church building | Time spent with people anywhere |
| Structure | Fluidity |
| Full schedule | Lots of white space |
| Total number of minutes | Total number of moments |

# How to Think Like an Entrepreneur

Although a certain percentage of people may be exceptionally creative and insightful, we firmly believe that everybody can raise the value of what they have or what they do by applying the same innovative principles that entrepreneurs use to raise the value of the assets at their disposal. Peter Drucker tells us:

> Innovation is the specific tool of entrepreneurs, the means by which they exploit change as an opportunity for a different business or a different service. It is capable of being presented as a discipline, capable of being learned, capable of being practiced. Entrepreneurs need to search purposefully for the sources of innovation, the changes and their symptoms that indicate opportunities for successful innovation. And they need to know and to apply the principles of successful innovation.[18]

How can we learn to think as entrepreneurs think? We suggest the following three ways of thinking.

## Look for Areas of Leverage to Make a Difference

Chip Sweney, from Perimeter Church in Atlanta, was visiting relatives in Colorado and dropped by my (Eric's) house one evening. As we sat on the back deck, Chip talked about a new ministry Perimeter had started, called "Half-Hour Heroes." Half-Hour Heroes are men and women who volunteer at a local public elementary or middle school for thirty minutes, once a week (often during lunchtime), as a tutor or just to be a friend to a student who could benefit from having a positive adult in their life. Chip said, "Our goal is that every child in metro Atlanta public schools in need of a mentor or tutor would have one."

Then Chip shared some interesting facts regarding the importance of this new ministry. "Did you know," he began, "that the percentage of students in metro Atlanta who are unable to attain reading proficiency by the third grade—30 percent—is directly proportionate to the number of students that do not graduate from high school?" Not reading by third grade is tied not only to graduation rate but also to teen pregnancy, drug use, and incarceration. In fact, Georgia bases its future prison population on the literacy rates of third graders. As one school administrator explained, "Up until third grade, you learn to read; after third grade, you read to learn." But there was more from Chip: "If a young person graduates high school, waits until age twenty before marrying, and has kids after they are married, the chance of living in poverty is a mere 8 percent. If any of these three factors is compromised, the chance of winding up in poverty increases tenfold—to 80 percent—so that's why we think what we are doing is important. If every student in need of an adult friend or a tutor had a Half-Hour Hero, we could help more students achieve success in life." Working with children is a leveraged activity that has multiple positive outcomes.

## Swim in the Blue Oceans

If we want to increase the value of what we do or come up with ideas that help us become the best church *for* the community, we have to learn to swim in "blue oceans." In 2005, W. Chan Kim and Renée Mauborgne published their best-selling book *Blue Ocean Strategy: How to Create Uncontested Market Space and Make Competition Irrelevant.* The authors talk about two colors of oceans that companies operate in. They write, "Red oceans represent all the industries in existence today. This is the known market space. Here companies try to outperform their rivals to grab a greater share of existing demand. As the market space gets crowded, prospects for profits and growth are reduced. Products become commodities, and cutthroat competition turns the red ocean bloody."

Blue oceans are different. "Blue oceans denote all the industries *not* in existence today. This is the unknown market space. . . . Blue oceans . . . demand creation and the opportunity for highly profitable growth."[19]

Churches, too, can swim in red oceans or blue oceans. Throughout this book, we have tried to distinguish between trying to be the best church *in* the community and trying to be the best church *for* the community. Trying to be the best church in the community puts you in competition with other local churches. You vie for market share in a red ocean. You differentiate by quality or style of worship, preaching, youth programs, and so on. There can only be one best church in the community. But by changing the preposition and striving to be the best church *for* your community, that changes everything. That becomes a blue-ocean strategy. There are no competitors; there is no competition. Every church can have this as its goal, and the community is the recipient of their collective efforts.

Jay Pathak, lead pastor at Vineyard Church in Arvada, Colorado, is no stranger to innovation. Several months ago Jay explained one of the church's blue-ocean strategies to me (Eric) over a cup of coffee:

> We start by asking, "What are the needs of the city?" not "What should we equip our people to do?" So, for example, about once a month, we go into a local bar in our community and ask [the owner or manager] to identify its slowest night for business. We then offer to bring a local band into the bar, split the gate with the owner, auction off live art, and sell CDs and T-shirts. We then take the money we raise and give it to local charities. We have raised thousands of dollars for local charities like Habitat for Humanity. It's a win all the way around. The bar makes a bit of money, and the local band gets publicity and often begins associating with the local charity it is helping sponsor. When people ask who we are, we tell them, "We're a group of people that have taken Jesus seriously, and we believe that Jesus cares about things like human trafficking, homeless people, children without clean water, and so on, and we're just trying to make a difference."

This is what it means to be the best church *for* the community. This is blue-ocean strategy.

## Look for the Unmet Need

To discover unmet needs in your community, the following exercise may be helpful. First, draw a Venn diagram as in figure 9.2. The three circles represent the needs of your community, your congregation's current engagement and capacity in your community, and what other congregations do well. Then simply start filling in the blanks. An exercise like this will help you identify not just opportunities to meet needs as a congregation but also what you can do to partner with other churches and others that love the city as you do.

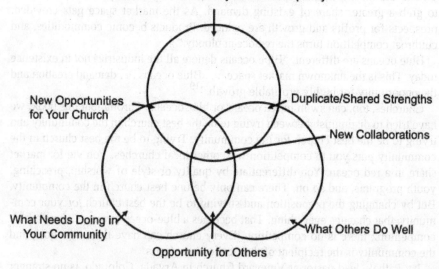

Your Church's Externally Focused Capacity

New Opportunities for Your Church

Duplicate/Shared Strengths

New Collaborations

What Needs Doing in Your Community

Opportunity for Others

What Others Do Well

## Pulling It All Together

God's act of creation was really the only original *ex nihilo* creative act. "For he spoke, and it came to be" (Ps 33:9). Everything else since that time has simply been rearranging the parts. Every color that you see is some combination of only three primary colors (yellow, blue, and red); every shape is a combination of three basic shapes (rectangles, circles, and triangles); and there are only three states of matter (solids, liquids, and gases).[20] The diversity of stars, planets, animals, vegetation, processes, and people attests to God's creativity. Since the time of creation, humans have simply rearranged the parts using existing materials. There is nothing new under the sun. Seen in that light, we don't have to be original to be creative. We simply need to bring different parts and pieces to the table and assemble them differently to serve our purpose.

The philosopher William James is said to have observed that "genius is the capacity for seeing relationships where lesser men see none."[21] By his own admission, Thomas Edison had only one completely original invention—the phonograph. Everything else was an adaptation of someone else's idea or discovery. He also purportedly advised, "Make it a practice to keep on the lookout for novel and interesting ideas that others have used successfully. Your idea has to be original only in its adaptation to the problem you are working on."[22]

Think of how many solutions or inventions have led to other creative solutions—the coin punch and wine press led to the invention of the printing press. How about surfboards and sailboats? The Gospel of Luke and movies? Skateboards and skis? How many other good ideas are waiting to be discovered simply by using the known to create usefulness in the arena of the unknown? What new breakthrough strategy is simply awaiting discovery?

A few years ago, we were talking with Pastor Laurie Beshore from Mariners Church about criteria for beginning a new ministry. She laughed when she told us about the latest ministry her church had launched—Mariners' Dog Ministry. Although Laurie initially wanted to dismiss the idea of a dog ministry, she was willing to try anything once. How can dogs be repurposed for ministry? Laurie went on to describe how dogs will calm crying children in the nursery, bringing peace where there had been chaos. Dogs are particularly good with the elderly and facilitate conversations—ask any single guy with a puppy in the park. Dog owners brought their dogs to the church summer camps, and the kids loved them. Dogs know nothing of social status and love everyone unconditionally. When the dogs show up at after-school programs, the children often prefer to read to a canine friend rather than to an adult! Each month, Mariners hosts birthday parties for residents in its motel ministry, and the dogs have been an integral part of the church's ministry to foster children. The dog ministry even has a mission: "To put people at ease and begin a process that could lead them to God." How do you combine dogs with ministry? Mariners has figured it out.

## Looking at the Same Thing … but Thinking Something Different

Several years ago, a good friend of mine (Eric's) packed up his family and moved to Spain to work on university campuses, winning students to Christ and helping them become ardent followers of Jesus. As John became more aware of the spiritual attitudes and hungers of Spaniards, he kept searching for ways to embrace the local culture and use what was at hand to begin spiritual conversations. Once a month, during the school year, John and his wife, Carrie, invited students into their home for supper. After supper, John would pass out reproductions of European paintings that depicted one of the many parables Jesus told. So, one night they might look at and discuss Rembrandt's *Return of the Prodigal* or Francesco Bassano's *Parable of the Good Samaritan*. After extracting all the visual clues in the painting, John would take the guests to the New Testament passage, and the discussion would begin anew. Many students who came to embrace Jesus began with dinner at John and Carrie's home.

In 1999, John and Carrie were thinking about how they could reach more people with the gospel. They heard of the *Camino de Santiago de Compostela* (The Way of Saint James)—a pilgrimage that has been going on for centuries in which the spiritually committed and spiritually curious trek across northern Spain to the city of Santiago de Compostela, in the northwest. The year 2000 was a special year of celebration, and an estimated one million people were going to walk at least some portion of the trail. Many evangelicals avoided the Camino like the plague. It wasn't part of their faith tradition. John, however, saw the same thing but thought something different: "Those who walk the trail are probably more spiritually open than those who stay home."

Every eight to ten miles along the pilgrim trail were *refugios*, or "pilgrim houses," where pilgrims could stop to rest, drink, eat, and sleep. John raised the money and bought one of these houses, refurbished it, and staffed it with European volunteers. He named the house *Fuente del Peregrino*—the Pilgrim's Fountain. But he did more. He bought five hundred Walkman cassette recorders (remember, this was before iPhones), and an hour east of *Fuente del Peregrino*, his volunteers handed out the Walkmans with a one-hour audio version of the *Jesus* film in one of several European languages. An hour later, they arrived at the pilgrim house, and many engaged in further conversations, some of which led to faith in Christ. Each night during the summer, they fed and housed thirty pilgrims, showed the *Jesus* film during the evening, and followed up with long conversations. Over the past twenty years, between the cassettes, literature, *Jesus* film, and personal conversations, the people in this pilgrim house have had a gospel influence on millions of people who have walked the Camino. To innovate, we must see the same things as those around us, but we must think about them differently.

## The Leadership Challenge

We noted at the beginning of this chapter that all leaders have at their disposal the same resources to accomplish their mission. How could you be entrepreneurial by repurposing how you use those resources to become the best church *for* your community? Think about what you need to do to shift each of the six resources—people, facilities, prayer, finances, technology, and time—to higher productivity and greater yield.

# 10.

## Outcomes: It's about the Game, Not the Pregame Talk

*Put me in coach, I'm ready to play . . . today*
*Look at me, gotta be, Centerfield.*

—John Fogerty, "Centerfield"

As the team finishes dressing, the head football coach calls them in to have a seat. Some players are looking intently at him with anticipation, while others sit with their elbows on their knees, fingers interlaced or tented. Many of them are nervously bouncing their heels off the floor. "You all know what day this is," the coach begins. "I don't need to tell you why you are here." He then launches into an inspiring homily on the theme of "courage against the odds." The speech is a barnburner—part William Wallace before his fellow Scotsmen, part Henry V before the Battle of Agincourt. Victory would be tough, but it was not out of their reach—if they would be courageous. As the speech ends, the team members rise to their feet and begin shouting; with helmets held high, they jump and chant in unison, "Win! Win! Win!" The coach revels in the response of the team. He holds both hands up to silence the men, and when he has their full attention, he ends with an admonition to "consider these things and take them to heart, and may the Lord add his blessing to what was said today." The team is dismissed, with many players telling the coach on the way out that his pregame speech was one of his very best. And then everyone goes home. Meanwhile, out on the field, where a game was waiting to be played and a battle to be won, the opponent is declared the victor by default.

Oblivious but satisfied with his performance, the coach goes home and starts preparing next week's pregame talk, on the topic "Luck favors the prepared." Meanwhile, back in the locker room, a lone player sits and asks himself, "If this was the pregame talk, what happened to the game? Why didn't we play the game?" The pregame talk is needed and appreciated, but the players long to play!

Is the story of the coach and his team really that different from what happens in churches all across our land? We often grade the service by how well the "pregame speech" went rather than by the performance of the team on the playing field. We are often long on exposition but come up short on application. Yet it is application that changes lives and changes the world. As the saying goes, "It is better to be ankle-deep in knowledge and neck-deep in application than neck-deep in knowledge and ankle-deep in application." As learners and gleaners of spiritual insight, we often want to be inspired more than we want to apply anything.

Leaders of externally focused churches think differently about what happens

141

when the team comes together. Like successful coaches, they understand that pregame speeches are good and useful, but only as they pertain to what people do once the speech is over and the team leaves the locker room and takes the field.

## Getting Everyone in the Game

Much of what is germane to getting everyone in the game can be found in chapter 7 and the structures necessary to making service an integral part of who you are as a church. Once we understand that every Christ-follower is created in Christ Jesus to do good works that God prepared in advance for that person (Eph 2:8–10), and that the leader's role is to prepare and equip those same people for those works of service (Eph 4:11–12), then it is fairly easy to grasp the fact that everyone needs to get in the game. What else can we do?

### Provide Regular Opportunities

The first thing you can do is *provide regular, easy-entry opportunities that give people the chance to change the world.* In the Leadership Challenge at the end of chapter 3, we talked about what success might look like. What if you measured your effectiveness not by attendance or budget but by something far greater? What if at the end of the year everyone in your faith community had a story to tell of how they had changed the world? For this to happen, the church would need to provide regular opportunities for people to engage the world in such a way that the world would be different because of their action. Wouldn't that be something?

We've already written extensively on one-day service events, but there are many other easy-entry opportunities. When Crossroads Church in Gwinnett County, Georgia, changed their name to 12Stone Church, they quickly introduced themselves to their community by launching "12days12ways"—as a creative way to help hurting people in Georgia. The public was able go online or to a kiosk at the Georgia Mall to nominate people and families in need. More than two hundred prizes were awarded, including two new Toyotas, a college scholarship, various Christmas gifts, a year's supply of gasoline, and a year's worth of groceries.[1] In 2019, after discovering that one in six children in Gwinnett County suffers from food insecurity, they launched Knockout Hunger (knockouthunger.com). Across their eight campuses they asked each 12Stone family to provide one day of meals for a family of five. Collectively, average people were able to provide almost 140,000 meals for their neighbors. They also were able to retire the school lunch debt of over nine thousand students in the metro Atlanta area.[2] Everybody gets to play.

Several Sunday mornings a month, my (Rick's) church invites people to sign up to be "gone for good." (If you're thinking there are some people you'd like to sign up for this, put the thought away; it's not that kind of "gone"!) Instead of coming into a worship service, people jump into a van and head to a short-term service project. They try to be back (not too sweaty or smelly) for the last service of the morning at 11:00 a.m. It is one of those "acts of kindness" or "living gracefully" service opportunities. People *leave* the service and *do* service. They are "gone for good" (gone to *do* good). Almost all of the "gone for good" projects are with partners in the community. For example, the local code enforcement agency has often called LifeBridge to assist shut-ins, single moms, or terminally ill residents who face code violations for lawn or snow issues around their homes. Volunteers show up and, in a few hours, clean up a yard, repair a fence, remove debris, or clear snow. Sometimes people assist a school with a maintenance project or help a single mom with moving issues. Anybody can be on these teams and get in the game.

A few years ago the people at Southbrook Christian Church in Miamisburg, Ohio, had ambitious plans. They wanted to finish the construction of an AIDS clinic in Swaziland and help struggling people in their own local community. But how do you accomplish more with less? These innovative leaders came up with what they called the "Southbrook Meltdown": they asked their crowd to donate unworn class rings and broken or unused gold and silver jewelry. Ramping up with teaching from James 5:1–6, an interview with a missionary doctor, a bit of media coverage, and a Brinks armored truck for effect during the weekend "meltdown" offering, they collected jewelry with a scrap value of more than $150,000. This is the entrepreneurial spirit that we wrote about in chapter 9. Southbrook literally took something of little value from a jewelry box or sock drawer and raised it to a level that would save lives. Everyone got to play.

## Create a Challenge

A great way to get more people in the game is through specific challenges. Challenges often bring out the best in people. To be effective, challenges must be *specific*, *doable*, and *time-bound*. Remember the powerful impact of the "Plus One" week that LifeBridge had? Specific, doable, and time-bound. Here are a couple of suggestions to get you started.

Remember the rhythm of "Believe, Belong, Bless" in chapter 3? What if you challenged everyone in your congregation to live out that simple rhythm for just thirty days, or maybe during the forty days of the Lenten season? Then have people tell and record their stories of what happened as a result of this experiment.

Another powerful kick-start might be to create some sort of challenge around Matthew 25:31–46: "For I was hungry and you gave me something to eat, I was thirsty and you gave me something to drink, I was a stranger and you invited me in, I needed clothes and you clothed me, I was sick and you looked after me, I was in prison and you came to visit me." What if every family unit or every small group was asked to figure out, within some specific time frame, a way to

- feed the hungry,
- give water to the thirsty,
- welcome the immigrant,

- clothe those who need clothing,
- take care of the sick, or
- visit the prisoner.

If this is not just a metaphor and these will be real questions Jesus will actually ask us one day, it would be awesome to have the right answer and help others have solid answers. This would be challenging, but doable. Could you imagine the transformation that might take place?

## Combine Opportunity with Inclination

"The step from inclination to action is a large one," note Samuel and Pearl Oliner, so a second way to get people involved is to *combine opportunity with inclination*. You've got to strike while the iron is hot. We love what happened at Fellowship Bible Church in Nashville, Tennessee, when they sent a team of 150 Fellowship members to Biloxi, Mississippi, to help victims of Hurricane Katrina. As they were distributing water, food, and clothing, one of the team members, Dave, met a man without shoes who needed a pair of work boots so he could clean up his home. After Dave learned that they wore the same size shoe, he took off his work boots and gave them to his new friend. The rest of the day, Dave worked in his socks. Like the famed "Shoeless" Joe Jackson, Dave was in the game. Dave had given his boots away to someone who needed them more than he did.

A few weeks later, Teaching Pastor Lloyd Shadrach projected images from a recent team trip to Africa. The pictures were unusual in that they focused on the feet of children wearing their parents' shoes. Lloyd then explained that children in this African village were not allowed to attend school unless they had shoes. So, their parents did what parents do: they gave their own shoes to their children so the youngsters could be educated. The parents would do their work barefoot. Lloyd now came to his application:

> There are adults and children in Africa who need a pair of shoes. There are children right here in Nashville that need a pair of shoes. There are adults and children in Peru, Honduras, Sudan, Nigeria, and Biloxi who need a pair of shoes. If I looked at any one of you in the eyes this morning and said, "Do you know there are people who need your shoes?" every one of us would say, "I know that!" Every one of us would say, "I believe that!" Here's the invitation. Let's go beyond that awareness. Let's do something right now—let's give them our shoes—now, in this moment. That's the invitation.[3]

Lloyd was combining inclination to give with the opportunity to give. He then bent down and took his shoes off and laid them on the stage. That morning, twenty-five hundred people got in the game and gave twenty-five hundred pairs of shoes to people who needed them. Imagine the evangelistic opportunities that occurred that week in and around Nashville as hundreds of people told their friends, neighbors, and coworkers, "My pastor asked us to do the craziest thing yesterday. . ."

On a beautiful spring day, Dennis Keating, lead pastor at Emanuel Faith Church in Escondido, California, started a multiweek series of messages designed to engage congregants in the needs of the world, titled, "God Cares, I Care." God cares about the hungry, the thirsty, the prisoners, orphans, the sick, the broken, the prodigal, and so on. Understanding that a person's motivation would not be higher than at the end of the message, each sermon concluded with an opportunity to do something right then and there about the need that was presented. People were asked specifically to give or to go out and help, and hundreds got into the game by responding. Following Dennis's message on God caring for the hungry, families donated more than 20,000 shopping bags of food to the local food bank.[4]

One weekend I (Rick) was preaching a message series on money and finances. In an attempt to illustrate how well-off we are as a society, I told a brief story about children in India:

> I met a man who was doing incredible work there. He was rescuing children from extreme poverty by purchasing them for less than $50 per child so the children could be returned to their families or placed in a caring home. Most of those children were being sold because their families couldn't afford to feed all their children. So, they would sell one to feed the others. Most of the children sold in this manner end up in the sex trade industry.

Afterward, I had people stuffing $50 in my hand to give to this man in India to purchase more children out of poverty and save them from a life of misery. One man came up and simply said, "I want to help," and handed me a check for $50,000. Ten minutes later, he returned with his wife and offered an additional $50,000.

That one story led to LifeBridge partnering with Central India Christian Mission to rescue children in several communities in India, to provide schools, orphanages, and church planting in those communities. God's people want to get in the game. We are always more fulfilled through contribution than we are by mere consumption.

## Make It Personal

A third essential is to *personally invite people to serve with you*. Don't expect general pleas to work. Although people serve for a number of reasons, including compelling need, surveys show that when somebody they respect asks them personally to serve together, the success rate is 93 percent.[5] The key words are "Come do this *with me*." Don Simmons points out that there are three *I*'s necessary for attracting and asking volunteers:

1. *Identify.* Identify the specific people who would do a great job serving others in this specific area.

2. *Inform.* Let people know what they are going to be doing if they join you in service. The worst thing you could say to them is "Just pitch in; you'll figure things out when you get there." Keep in mind that this is about

equipping, not just recruiting.

3. *Invest.* Give people a chance to try it out before they commit for the long term. An honest no is way better than a dishonest yes.

Your role is to put people in service and to help them discover their unique place and contribution. These people are serving, not just volunteering. Ministering to them is perhaps more important than the ministry of service they are doing.

Inviting others personally takes time, effort, and energy, but it can be effective if it is focused on their growth and development. What if your staff, elders, or leaders simply modeled an easy-entry point like that and asked one person to go along with them to serve? How many more would get in the game?

### Begin with the Willing

In getting people into the game, it is important to recognize that not everybody initially wants to play. That's OK. It is helpful to understand that you don't have to persuade and enlist everyone, or even the majority, before you can begin an externally focused initiative. You can just *work with the willing*—the early adopters, the early enthusiasts—and let them create the working models and position them to tell the stories that will spread to the rest of the folk. (For a fuller explanation of this concept, Google "Diffusion of Innovations" by Everett Rogers or "Crossing the Chasm" by Geoffrey Moore.) The point is that nearly everyone can be persuaded to embrace new ideas, but people need various amounts of information and time before they are comfortable accepting something new and being willing to serve. So, realistically, creating systems where everyone is enthusiastically engaged will take some time. But be patient. You are in this for the long haul! Remember the words of Thomas Paine: "Time makes more converts than reason."[6]

## How to Tell If You Are "Winning"

It is one thing to get everybody playing, but how do we determine the score? How do we measure whether we are winning or not? Measuring begins with mission. Mission is the only solid standard against which you can measure progress.

A few years ago, Jim Collins produced a little thirty-five-page gem titled *Good to Great and the Social Sectors.* Collins writes:

For a business, financial returns are a perfectly legitimate measure of performance. For a social sector organization, however, performance must be relative to mission, not financial returns. In the social sectors, the critical question is not "How much money do we make per dollar of invested capital?" but "How effectively do we deliver on our mission and make a distinctive impact, relative to our resources?"

It really doesn't matter whether you can quantify your results. What matters is that you rigorously assemble evidence—quantitative or qualitative—to track your progress. If the evidence is primarily qualitative, think like a trial lawyer assembling the combined body of evidence. If the evidence is primarily quantitative, then think of yourself as a laboratory scientist assembling and assessing the data.[7]

The important thing is to decide what you will consistently keep track of to know whether you are making progress against the goal and above your baseline. As an example of consistent measurement, Collins cites the Cleveland Orchestra. How does one measure the progress or excellence of an orchestra? Its expressed goal was "artistic excellence," but that was too subjective, so the director, Tom Morris, came up with a scorecard that would provide indicators of artistic excellence. The orchestra would measure six things:[8]

1. Number of standing ovations
2. Number of complex pieces the orchestra can play with excellence
3. Number of invitations from Europe's most prestigious music festivals
4. Number of tickets sold
5. Number of other orchestras that mimic Cleveland Orchestra's style
6. Number of composers who want their work debuted in Cleveland

If your goal is to become the best church *for* the community rather than the best church *in* the community, the scorecard for what you measure must change. This is not to suggest that you stop counting the offering or the weekend attendance, but if you really want to be the best church *for* the community, you need to come up with additional measurements.

Dan Nold, senior pastor at Calvary Baptist Church in State College, Pennsylvania, changed the church's scorecard to reflect the church's missional commitment. Dan now counts four new things they had not counted before:

1. Number of community partnerships
2. Number of people to whom the church is providing food
3. Number of small groups consistently serving in the community
4. Number of community-centered God stories

What would you add to Dan's list? Following the lead of our musical counterparts from Cleveland, what might the church creatively measure to gauge its effectiveness in accomplishing its missional goals? Here are a few ideas:

- Number of favorable articles about the church in the local newspaper
- Number of other church leaders who want to see "what you do and how you do it"
- Number of awards you get from the community
- Number of church-community partnerships listed in the church bulletin

After reading *The Externally Focused Church*, Pastor Jeff Valentine of Missoula Alliance Church (MAC) in Missoula, Montana, went to the principal of a local elementary school and asked if MAC could supply some tutors for the kids. The principal, probably thinking about church-and-state issues, was cautious. It would be OK if the church sent three tutors. Soon the three tutors became nine tutors as the positive effects on the kids' lives became evident. This particular school has a number of children whose parents are addicted to crack cocaine. Any money coming into the home goes toward crack, and the ones who suffer for it are the kids. So, for the Christmas Eve service, Jeff asked the people of MAC to give generously, disclosing that half of the offering would go to the school to spend on children in need.

The following week, the principal received a check for $14,000. He and his team could spend the money on students in distress—money the school just didn't have before. So, between shoes, clothing, dental care, and supplies, MAC gave the opportunity for the principal to be a blessing to his students. Unsolicited, the principal put out a press release about what MAC did, and the article made the front page of the local newspaper. Copies of the article were included with every school employee's paycheck.

And there is more to the story. The principal, initially so hesitant about working with a church, now openly embraces MAC's efforts. Together, MAC and the school are making a tangible difference in the lives of children. MAC's vision is to help Missoula become the healthiest community in the state of Montana. It's not about the church; it's about the city, about the kingdom. MAC's measurement of success looks amazingly different today from how it looked just a few years ago.

## Expanding the Church Scorecard

A few years ago, W. David Phillips posted an entry on his blog titled "Measuring Success in Ministry." David reflected on a question Len Sweet had posed in his doctoral class regarding "metaphors that will describe how we measure success in the church in the future." Eschewing the traditional measurements of how many, how often, and how much, here is the list the class (with a few later additions from David) came up with:

1. The number of cigarette butts in the church parking lot
2. The number of adoptions people in the church have made from local foster care
3. The number of pictures on the church wall of unwed mothers holding their newborn babies in their arms for the first time
4. The number of classes for special needs children and adults
5. The number of former convicted felons serving in the church
6. The number of phone calls from community leaders asking the church's advice

7. The number of meetings that take place somewhere besides the church building

8. The number of organizations using the church building

9. The number of days the pastor doesn't spend time in the church office but in the community

10. The number of emergency finance meetings that take place to reroute money to community ministry

11. The amount of dollars saved by the local schools because the church has painted the walls

12. The number of people serving in the community during the church's normal worship hours

13. The number of non-religious-school professors worshipping with you

14. The number of people wearing good, free clothes that used to belong to members of the church

15. The number of times the church band has played family-friendly music in the local coffee shop

16. The number of people who have gotten better because of the free health clinic you operate

17. The number of people in new jobs thanks to the free job-training center you opened

18. The number of microloans given by members in your church

19. The number of churches your church planted in a 10-mile radius of your own church[9]

## The Flourishing Community Scorecard

What if you expanded your scorecard to changes in your community? What if you aligned your impacts with God's impacts? When God has the chance to build a city from scratch—the new Jerusalem (Isa 65:18–25)—what kind of city will that be? What is God's view of human flourishing? The city is a place of

- forward-looking people (v. 17);
- gladness, delight, joy and well-being (vv. 18–19);
- physical health and longevity (v. 20);
- housing and food security (v. 21);
- meaningful, enjoyable and rewarding work (v. 22);
- upward generational mobility (v. 23);

- strong, intergenerational family structure (v. 23);
- child welfare (v. 23);
- spiritual community (v. 24);
- reconciliation (v. 25);
- absence of violence and peace (v. 25).

What if the characteristics found in Isaiah 65 served as the metrics of the outcomes you were pursuing? In 2016, Harvard University founded their Human Flourishing Program to discover and promote the factors that lead to human flourishing. Led by Dr. Tyler VanderWeele, they discovered that human flourishing consists of six characteristics:

- Happiness and life satisfaction
- Physical and mental health
- Meaning and purpose
- Character and virtue
- Close social relationships
- Financial and material stability

They look a bit like Isaiah 65, don't they? VanderWeele defines flourishing as "a state in which all aspects of a person's life are good."[10] VanderWeele and his colleagues discovered that the "prominent pathways to human flourishing" are

- family,
- work,
- education, and
- religious community.

VanderWeele notes that "if efforts [were made] to support, improve, and promote participation in these pathways, the consequences for human flourishing would be substantial."[11] VanderWeele's diagram (see figure 10.1) suggests, and his research verifies, that your faith community greatly influences every one of the flourishing outcomes of people in your city as well as the other pathways to that flourishing.

What could your church offer in the "family" pathway? VanderWeele's study concludes that marriage is associated with "higher levels of positive relationships with others, higher levels of perceived social support, . . . lower levels of loneliness, . . . [and] happier children." He concludes, "The effects of marriage on health, happiness and life satisfaction, meaning and purpose, character and virtue, close social relationships, and financial stability are thus profound."[12]

How could your church influence the workplace? Could Christian business owners learn to "pastor" their work force? Could 10 percent of new jobs be reserved for the most vulnerable? Could your church be engaged in education through improving third-grade reading levels? We encourage you to follow Harvard's Human Flourishing Program to learn more about the role you and your church can play in creating a thriving community. Nothing changes until the scorecard changes.

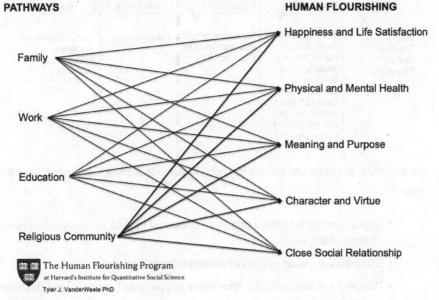

Figure 10.1

## The Externally Focused Scorecard—the Logic Model

Five familiar words represent concepts that are important in creating an externally focused scorecard. These words—*inputs, activities, outputs, outcomes,* and *impact*—are familiar to most nonprofit agencies but are not usually part of the vocabulary of the local church. The causal relationship between the words and their underlying concepts is shown in figure 10.2.

# What is your "Score Card?"—The Logic Model

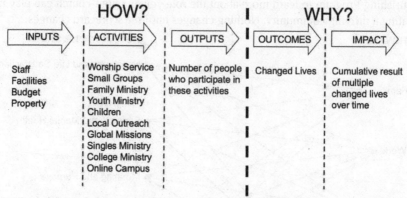

Are the inputs, activities, and outputs the right elements to produce outcomes & impact?

Figure 10.2

- *Inputs* are the resources that were dedicated to your ministry—facilities, budget, staff, etc.

- *Activities* are what you do to accomplish your mission.

- *Outputs* are measured by how many people you have involved in those activities.

- *Outcomes* are the short- and medium-range changes that occurred in individual lives or families. Peter Drucker insists that the bottom line for all nonprofit organizations is always "changed human beings."[13]

- *Impact* is the long-range change in the community, society, or environment that is the result of multiple changed lives over time—a flourishing city.

*Outcomes* and *impact* answer the questions "So what?" or "What difference did the inputs, activities, and outputs make in the lives of others?"

Here's an important insight: If you ask a pastor or leader to describe their church, the answer will usually be related to inputs, activities, or outputs:

- *Inputs:* "We have twenty-eight full-time staff and a fifteen-hundred-seat auditorium that sits on twenty-five acres just north of the city."

- *Activities:* "We have three morning services, a full Sunday school program, over fifty small groups, and . . ."

- *Outputs:* "We attract around fifteen hundred in weekend worship, three hundred in Sunday school, and over seven hundred people in small groups . . ."

And that is where the measurement stops. We must remember, however, that we measure what matters by measuring *outcomes* and *impact*. Inputs, activities, and outputs are always in service to outcomes and impact. Never lose sight of the fact that outcomes and impact answer the questions "So what?" and "What difference did it make?" *Outcomes* specify the changes that occurred in individuals as the result of your activities. *Impact* refers to the long-term changes that are the collective results of the changes of individuals. We define externally focused churches as churches that measure their effectiveness not only by the number of people in the weekend service (output) but also by the transformational effect the church is having on the community (outcomes and impact).

Our friends at Bethel Church in Richland, Washington, told us a story that illustrates the relationship between activities and outcomes:

> Through Bethel's car repair ministry, which is called Elijah's Pit Stop (an *activity*), a formerly homeless drug addict has learned to be a mechanic (*outcome*) and is rapidly learning to handle a wide array of administrative functions (*outcome*). Kenny is now working thirty to thirty-five hours per week for Elijah's and five to ten hours per week for the commercial car repair shop that donates repair bay space to Elijah's every other Saturday. Kenny now has a wife, an apartment, and a car (*outcome*). He is also becoming adept at mentoring other homeless people, as well as struggling young men from single-parent homes (*outcome* and *impact*). Kenny is now helping others flourish.

What is your scorecard? What does "winning" look like? How do you measure what really counts in your life and in your church? When you describe your church, do you talk in terms of *inputs* (size of staff, budget, and facility), *activities* (the list of Bible studies, ministries, and programs), and *outputs* (number of people who attended your events, program, or activities) or in terms of *outcomes* and *impacts* (changed lives and flourishing communities)? If you are not seeing the desirable *outcomes* and *impact*, you must adjust your *inputs*, *activities*, and *outputs*. As we've said many times, becoming the best church *for* the community is a different game than wanting to become the best church *in* the community. You will need new skills, new eyes, and new, like-minded companions to help you on this new journey. But we assure you that it will be worth it, and you'll have the time of your life.

## The Leadership Challenge

We've come to the end of the book but possibly the beginning of a new adventure and direction for your life and ministry. We thoroughly believe that our best years are still ahead of us and that your best years are ahead of you. We leave you with the following questions to think about and answer:

- What would your community look like if all Christ-followers were engaged in meeting the needs and dreams of the community?
- What could you do to get everybody in the game?

- What does your scorecard look like?

- What do you want to measure?

- How can you build human flourishing into your scorecard?

- What can you do to help people discover their Ephesians 2:10 intersection of passion and purpose?

- How could you structure church so that at the end of the year, every person had a story to tell of how, in ways great or small, he or she had changed the world?

# Notes

## Preface

1. Martin Luther King Jr., "I've Been to the Mountaintop," speech delivered Apr. 3, 1968, Mason Temple, Memphis, Tenn.
2. John Fitzgerald Kennedy, inaugural address delivered Jan. 20, 1961, Washington, D.C.

## Chapter 1
## What Kind of Day Is Today?

1. David Smith, *Mission after Christendom* (London: Darton, Longman & Todd, 2003), ix.
2. Elon University School of Communications, "Imagining the Internet," accessed February 27, 2020, https://tinyurl.com/ldmzbcl.
3. Joe McKinley, "13 Predictions about the Future That Were Dead Wrong," *Reader's Digest*, accessed February 27, 2020, https://tinyurl.com/rn3gznx.
4. Louis Menand, "Everybody's an Expert: Putting Predictions to the Test," *New Yorker*, November 28, 2005, https://tinyurl.com/cjn72n.
5. Megan Brenan, "Nurses Again Outpace Other Professions for Honesty, Ethics," Gallup, December 20, 2018, https://tinyurl.com/w5sq694.
6. Barna Group, *Barna Trends 2018: What's New and What's Next at the Intersection of Faith and Culture* (Grand Rapids: Baker, 2017), 116.
7. Bob Goff, *Love Does: Discover a Secretly Incredible Life in an Ordinary World* (Nashville, TN: Thomas Nelson, 2012), 82.
8. Tim Newman, "Anxiety in the West: Is It on the Rise?" *Medical News Today*, September 5, 2018, https://tinyurl.com/wbkrm7n.
9. Megan Fowler, "The Bible App's Most Popular Verse of 2019: 'Do Not Worry,'" *Christianity Today*, December 9, 2019, https://tinyurl.com/wx2ot2l.
10. Newman, "Anxiety in the West."
11. Zack Friedman, "Student Loan Debt Statistics in 2019: A $1.5 Trillion Crisis," *Forbes*, February 25, 2019, https://tinyurl.com/uh37t8g.
12. Shamard Charles, "Social Media Linked to Rise in Mental Health Disorders, Survey Finds," *NBC News*, March 14, 2019, https://tinyurl.com/yyytqgtb.
13. Barna Group, *Reviving Evangelism: Current Realities That Demand a New Vision for Sharing Faith.* 2019.

14. Barna Group, "Only One-Third of Young Adults Feels Cared For by Others," October 15, 2019, https://tinyurl.com/yx5hm6rx.

15. Andrew Thompson, "Google's Mission Statement and Vision Statement (An Analysis," Panmore Institute, February 13, 2019, https://tinyurl.com/zo4a689.

16. Thompson, "Google's Mission Statement and Vision Statement."

17. Barna, *Barna Trends 2018*, 29.

18. Kashmir Hill, "How Target Figured Out a Teen Girl Was Pregnant before Her Father Did," *Forbes*, February 16, 2012, https://tinyurl.com/wvnsllz.

19. Tiffany Hsu, "You See Pepsi, I See Coke: New Tricks for Product Placement," *New York Times*, December 20, 2019, https://tinyurl.com/s5n2qdl.

20. Mansoor Iqbal, "App Download and Usage Statistics (2019)," Business of Apps, November 19, 2019, https://tinyurl.com/y4rpc5gx.

21. Darina Lynkova, "The Surprising Reality of How Many Emails Are Sent per Day," TechJury, April 22, 2019, https://tinyurl.com/ww2t9qc.

22. Megan Morreale, "Daily SMS Mobile Usage Statistics," SMSEagle, March 6, 2017, https://tinyurl.com/yyofarnd.

23. Conversation between Eric Swanson (author) and Grant Skeldon, in Boulder Colorado, December 31, 2019.

24. "Television Consumption," Wikipedia, last edited February 3, 2020, https://tinyurl.com/s6m27qj.

25. Amanda Luz Henning Santiago, "361,000 Americans Binge-Watched the Entire Second Season of Netflix's 'Stranger Things' in the First 24 Hours, Nielsen Says," *Business Insider*, November 2, 2017, https://tinyurl.com/wh79yue.

26. "The State of Online Gaming – 2019," Limelight Networks, accessed February 27, 2020, https://tinyurl.com/y2cekfk6.

27. Sheila Eugenio, "8 Cognitive Benefits of Playing Video Games for Kids," Engadget, February 9, 2017, https://tinyurl.com/yb6ohkjm.

28. Mark Wilson, "Chance the Rapper," *Fast Company*, November 18, 2019, https://tinyurl.com/wefsjfj.

29. John Lynch and Travis Clark, "A 7-Year-Old Boy Is Making $22 Million a Year Reviewing Toys on YouTube," *Business Insider*, December 3, 2018, https://tinyurl.com/y8t8kzy7.

30. "Black Swan Theory," Wikipedia, accessed March 16, 2020 https://tinyurl.com/ppezq9c.

31. Caleb Silver, "The Top 20 Economies in the World," Investopedia, November 19, 2019, https://tinyurl.com/y2f53utd.

32. Daniel H. Pink, *A Whole New Mind: Why Right-Brainers Will Rule the Future* (New York: Riverhead, 2006), 33.

33. Thomas L. Friedman, "Doing Our Homework," *New York Times*, June 24, 2004, https://tinyurl.com/u7smepx.

34. TJ McCue, "57 Million U.S. Workers Are Part of the Gig Economy," *Forbes*, August 31, 2018, https://tinyurl.com/ra5s64u.

35. "No one is as smart of all of us," Chief Learning Officer, December 2, 2019, https://tinyurl.com/uqm7ypf.

36. Eric S. Raymond, *The Cathedral and the Bazaar: Musings on Linux and Open Source by an Accidental Revolutionary* (Sebastopol, CA: O'Reilly Media, 2001), 30.

37. Innocentive website, accessed February 27, 2020, innocentive.com.

38. Tom Goodwin, "The Battle Is for the Customer Interface," TechCrunch, March 3, 2015, https://tinyurl.com/n95u4ua.

39. Eric Swanson, "Is Your Church a Pipeline, Portal or Platform?" *Christianity Today*, accessed February 27, 2020, https://tinyurl.com/wmw84tf.

40. Lawrence Gregory, "Amazon.com Inc.'s Misstion Statement and Vision Statement (An Analysis)," Panmore Institute, February 13, 2019, https://tiny url.com/ttl6q5a.

41. Mary Hanbury, "50 Haunting Photos of Abandoned Shopping Malls across America," *Business Insider*, November 8, 2019, https://tinyurl.com/t9kdfrt.

42. Jessica Dickler, "More Americans Say They Don't Carry Cash," CNBC, January 15, 2019, https://tinyurl.com/y79jtfc6.

43. Harrison Jacobs, "One Photo Shows That China Is Already a Cashless Future," *Business Insider*, May 29, 2018, https://tinyurl.com/syl8pyq.

44. "6 Reasons Your Church Should Regularly Promote Automated Recurring Giving," Tithe.ly, February 9, 2016, https://tinyurl.com/sowrhnn.

45. Fareed Zakaria, *The Post American World* (New York: Norton, 2008), 98, quoting Josepha Kahn and Jim Yardley, "As China Roars, Pollution Reaches Deadly Extremes," *New York Times*, Aug. 26, 2007.

46. Living Water International, "The Water Crisis," https://www.water.cc/aboutlivingwater.

47. Nicholas Mallos, "The Problem with Plastics," Ocean Conservancy, accessed February 27, 2020, https://tinyurl.com/y9vwmv6g.

48. Samuel Stebbins, "Worst Natural Disasters in the US in the Last 10 Years," 24/7 Wall St., September 24, 2019, https://tinyurl.com/v99lrcy.

49. Stebbins, "Worst Natural Disasters."

50. Jennifer Robison, "Millennials Worry about the Environment—Should Your Company?" Gallup, May 29, 2019, https://tinyurl.com/vlcq7fe.

51. Anthea Butler, "White Evangelicals Love Trump and Aren't Confused about Why. No One Should Be," NBC, September 27, 2019, https://tinyurl.com/yyswoay5.

52. Nathan L. Gonzales, "The Stunningly Static Evangelical White Vote," Roll Call, November 17, 2014, https://tinyurl.com/rhppol3.

53. Jim Wallis, *God's Politics: Why the Right Gets It Wrong and the Left Doesn't Get It* (San Francisco: HarperSan Francisco, 2006), 8.

54. "Edward Gibbon," Wikiquote, accessed February 27, 2020, https://tinyurl.com/rloqjcd.

55. Aaron Earles, "Small, Struggling Congregations Fill U.S. Church Landscape," Lifeway Research, March 6, 2019, https://tinyurl.com/yxw6lrrx.

56. "Church Dropouts Have Risen to 64 Percent—But What about Those Who Stay?" Barna, September 4, 2019, https://tinyurl.com/wjkb3m3.

57. Rachel Held Evans, "Why Millennials Are Leaving the Church," CNN, July 27, 2013, https://tinyurl.com/u9z4962.

58. Grant Skeldon, *The Passion Generaton: The Seemingly Reckless, Definitely Disruptive, but Far from Hopeless Millennials* (Grand Rapids: Zondervan, 2018), 32.

59. Skeldon, *The Passion Generaton*, 23.

60. Baylor Religion Survey, *American Values, Mental Health and Using Technology in the Age of Trump*, Baylor University, September 2017, https://tinyurl.com/smrnh2n.

61. Rich Nathan, Twitter post, 5:28 AM, December 13, 2019, https://tinyurl.com/tqhyqya.

62. Tyler VanderWeele, "Religion and Health: New Empirical Research" (lecture presented at Harvard Lectures That Last 2015), YouTube, June 23, 2015, https://tinyurl.com/wrx8l3j.

63. George Barna and David Kinneman, *Churchless: Understanding Today's Unchurched and How to Connect with Them* (Grand Rapids: Tyndale Momentum, 2016), 158.

64. Smith, *Mission after Christendom*, 35.

65. R. T. Kendal, *Unashamed to Bear His Name* (Bloomington, MN: Chosen Books, 2012), 133.

# Chapter 2
## Focus: They Choose the Window Seat, Not the Aisle Seat

1. John P. Schuster, *Answering Your Call: A Guide for Living Your Deepest Purpose* (San Francisco: Berrett-Koehler, 2003), Kindle locations 235–38.

2. Rodney Stark, *The Rise of Christianity: How the Obscure, Marginal Jesus Movement Became the Dominant Religious Force in the Western World in a Few Centuries* (San Francisco: HarperOne, 1997), 6.

3. David Bosch, *Transforming Mission* (Maryknoll, NY: Orbis, 1991), 49. The quotation is from Adolf von Harnack, *The Mission and Expansion of Christianity in the First Three Centuries*, vol. 1 (New York: Harper, 1908).

4. Thomas Massaro, *Living Justice: Catholic Social Teaching in Action* (Lanham, MD: Rowman & Littlefield, 2000), 14–15.

5. Attributed to Vance Havner (1901–1986), the "Dean of American Revival Preachers," a source of numerous *bons mots*.

6. Ram A. Cnaan et al., *The Invisible Caring Hand: American Congregations and the Provision of Welfare* (New York: New York University Press, 2002), 10.

7. Thom S. Rainer, "Seven Sins of Dying Churches," *Outreach*, January–February 2006, 16.

8. Ron Seller, "Churches Tend to See Missions and Ministry as the Same," Facts and Trends, January/February 2007, 9, https://tinyurl.com/vkm4nec.

9. Eric Swanson, *Ten Paradigm Shifts toward Community Transformation* (Dallas: Leadership Network, 2003).
10. Swiss Brethren Conference, "The Schleitheim Confession," adopted February 24, 1527 (Crockett, KY: Rod & Staff, 1985), https://tinyurl.com/wzzthgc.
11. Bosch, *Transforming Mission*, 318.
12. Diana R. Garland, "Church Social Work," in *Christianity and Social Work: Readings on the Integration of Christian Faith and Social Work Practice*, ed. Beryl Hugen (Botsford, CT: North American Association of Christians in Social Work, 1998), 22.
13. Community Foundation Serving Boulder County, *Quality of Life in Boulder County, 2005: A Community Indicators Report* (Boulder, CO: Community Foundation, 2005).
14. Ram A. Cnaan, Robert J. Wineburg, and Stephanie C. Boddie, *The Newer Deal: Social Work and Religion in Partnership* (New York: Columbia University Press, 1999), 51.
15. "Missing the Nature of Religious Faith" (editorial), *Toronto Star*, August 24, 2007, https://tinyurl.com/wx8netk.
16. Robert D. Lupton, *Theirs Is the Kingdom: Celebrating the Gospel in Urban America*, ed. Barbara R. Thompson (San Francisco: HarperOne, 1989), 60–61.
17. Reggie McNeal, *The Present Future: Six Tough Questions for the Church* (San Francisco: Jossey-Bass, 2009), 32.
18. Adam Hochschild, *Bury the Chains: Prophets and Rebels in the Fight to Free an Empire's Slaves* (New York: Houghton Mifflin, 2005), 29.
19. Hochschild, *Bury the Chains*, 29.
20. Hochschild, *Bury the Chains*, 77.
21. Rick Warren, comments, HIV/AIDS Summit, Saddleback Church, Lake Forest, CA, November 29, 2005.

# Chapter 3
# Purpose: They Practice Weight Training, Not Bodybuilding

1. Alan Roxburgh, comments, Dallas Seminary Missional Church Conference, Dallas, TX, April 1, 2008.
2. Abraham H. Maslow, "A Theory of Human Motivation," *Psychological Review* 50 (1943): 370–96.
3. Tim Kennedy, "Musana Children's Home," YouTube, October 7, 2008, https://tinyurl.com/sfgszj2.
4. Tim Kennedy, "Musana Children's Home."
5. Elie Wiesel, *Night* (New York: Hill & Wang, 2006), 120.
6. Bob Roberts Jr., "Power of the 'Glocal' Church," *Rev!*, September–October 2008, 138.
7. "Our Mission," Hope of the Poor, accessed February 28, 2020, hopeofthepoor.org.

8. Baylor University School of Social Work, "The Role of Faith in the Service of Christian Volunteers," Center for Family & Community Ministries, 2006, https://tinyurl.com/spo5cvh.

9. Kevin G. Ford, *Transforming Church: Bringing Out the Good to Get to Great* (Colorado Springs, CO: Cook, 2008), 32.

10. Michael E. Sherr, Diana R. Garland, Dennis R. Meyers, and Terry A. Wolfer, "Community Ministry Powerful Factor in Maturing Teens' Faith," Baylor University Media and Public Relations, January 22, 2007, https://tinyurl.com/yx8xwd4k.

11. Thom S. Rainer and Sam S. Rainer III, *Essential Church? Reclaiming a Generation of Dropouts* (Nashville, TN: B&H, 2008), 155.

12. "Minimum viable product," Wikipedia, https://tinyurl.com/qsd2fuc.

13. Jay Yarow, "The Zappos Founder Just Told Us All Kinds of Crazy Stories —Here's the Suprisingly Candid Interview," *Business Insider*, November 28, 2011, https://tinyurl.com/w76r83b.

14. BJ Fogg, "Forget Big Change, Start with a Tiny Habit," TEDx (Freemont, CA), posted December 5, 2012, https://tinyurl.com/q7veuch.

15. We owe this insight to a conversation between Eric Swanson (author) and Geoffrey Hsu, formerly with Campus Crusade for Christ, who was struggling to come up with a replacement watchword for Campus Crusade's "Win, Build, Send" approach to college students. Geoffrey argues that today's students are more attracted to the idea of "Believe, belong, and bless." He currently serves as executive director of Flourish San Diego.

# Chapter 4
## Story: They Live in the Kingdom Story, Not a Church Story

1. Tim Keller, "What Is Jesus' Mission?" *Gospel Christianity*, course 1, unit 7 (New York: Redeemer Presbyterian Church, 2003), 4.

2. Daniel Pink, *A Whole New Mind: Why Right-Brainers Will Rule the World* (New York: Riverhead, 2006), 102.

3. Michael Frost and Alan Hirsh, *The Shaping of Things to Come: Innovation and Mission for the 21st-Century Church* (Peabody, MA: Hendrickson, 2003), 33.

4. E. Stanley Jones, *The Unshakable Kingdom and the Unchanging Person* (Nashville, TN: Abingdon, 1972), 30.

5. Howard Snyder, *Liberating the Church* (Downers Grove, IL: InterVarsity, 1983), 11.

6. N. T. Wright, *Simply Christian: Why Christianity Makes Sense*, 9th ed. (San Francisco: HarperOne, 2006).

7. Pink, *Whole New Mind*, 102.

8. Bob Moffitt, *If Jesus Were Mayor* (Phoenix: Harvest, 2004), 10.

9. Bob Roberts Jr., "Power of the 'Glocal' Church," *Rev!*, September–October 2008, 138.

## Chapter 5
## Missions: The Few Sending the Many, Not the Many Sending the Few

1. David Smith, *Mission after Christendom* (London: Darton, Longman & Todd, 2003), 78.
2. David Neff, "Global Is the New Local," *Christianity Today*, June 2009, 39.
3. Neff, "Global Is the New Local."
4. Philip Jenkins, *The Next Christendom: The Coming of Global Christianity* (New York: Oxford University Press, 2002), 1.
5. Jenkins, *The Next Christendom*, 2.
6. David A. Livermore, *Serving with Eyes Wide Open: Doing Short-Term Missions with Cultural Intelligence* (Grand Rapids, MI: Baker, 2006), 33.
7. Jenkins, *The Next Christendom*, 71.
8. Jenkins, *The Next Christendom*, 71.
9. Rob Moll, "Missions Incredible," *Christianity Today*, March 1, 2006, 28, https://tinyurl.com/st44nrb.
10. Livermore, *Serving with Eyes Wide Open*, 40.
11. William Gibson, quoted in "Books of the Year," *Economist*, December 4, 2003, https://tinyurl.com/qkmspx5.
12. Desmond Tutu, Brainy Quotes, https://tinyurl.com/vecopjy.
13. Matt Olthoff, personal interview with the Eric Swanson, March 17, 2009.
14. Allen White, "What Is Rooted?" November 27, 2018, https://tinyurl.com/rzqgqja.
15. Scott White, personal interview with the Eric Swanson, May 5, 2009.
16. Tim Senff, personal interview with Eric Swanson, March 10, 2009.
17. Tom Mullis, personal interview with Eric Swanson, March 17, 2009.
18. Olthoff, personal interview.
19. Bob Roberts Jr., *Glocalization: How Followers of Jesus Engage a Flat World* (Grand Rapids, MI: Zondervan, 2007), 137.
20. Keith West, personal interview with Eric Swanson, June 16, 2009.
21. Durwood Snead, personal interview with Eric Swanson, May 6, 2009.
22. Eric Hanson, personal interview with Eric Swanson, April 8, 2009.
23. Steve Hanson, personal interview with Eric Swanson, June 25, 2009.
24. Quoted in Timothy C. Morgan, "Purpose Driven in Rwanda," *Christianity Today*, September 23, 2005, https://tinyurl.com/sr2jppg.
25. Saddleback Church, "The PEACE Plan," https://tinyurl.com/ycveqac2.
26. Rick Warren, "After the Aloha Shirts," *Christianity Today*, October 1, 2008, https://tinyurl.com/qr6qqye.
27. S. Hanson, personal interview.
28. Neff, "Global Is the New Local," 39.
29. Mike Robinson, personal interview with Eric Swanson, March 17, 2009.
30. See Jonathan Martin, *Giving Wisely: Killing with Kindness or Empowering Lasting Transformation?* (Redmond, OR: Last Chapter, 2008).

31. Snead, personal interview.

32. Dave Hall, personal interview with Eric Swanson, May 7, 2009.

33. Joey Shaw, personal interview with Eric Swanson, Mar. 24, 2009.

34. S. White, personal interview.

35. Mark Russell, *The Missional Entrepreneur: Principles and Practice for Business as Mission* (Birmingham, AL: New Hope, 2010), 185.

36. Neil Hendershot, personal interview with Eric Swanson, June 17, 2009.

37. Ian Stevenson, personal interview with Eric Swanson, March 10, 2009.

38. David Thoresen, personal interview with Eric Swanson, May 5, 2009.

39. Senff, personal interview.

40. *Built to Last: Successful Habits of Visionary Companies*, Good to Great series (New York: HarperBusiness, 1994).

41. "Global Media Outreach Reaches Milestone," Global Media Outreach, November 19, 2018, https://tinyurl.com/qtnybs8.

# Chapter 6
# Partnering: They Build Wells, Not Walls

1. Paul G. Hiebert, "Conversion, Culture and Cognitive Categories," *Gospel in Context* 1, no. 4 (1978): 24–29.

2. Michael Frost and Alan Hirsch, *The Shaping of Things to Come* (Peabody, MA: Hendrickson, 2004), 47.

3. *Reviving Evangelism: Current Realities That Demand a New Vision for Sharing Faith* (Barna Group, 2019), 23.

4. Quoted in Krista Petty, "Church-to-Church Collaborations on the Rise," Leadership Network, 2009, https://tinyurl.com/mekq46x.

5. Helen Lee, "Missional Shift or Drift?" *Christianity Today*, November 7, 2008, https://tinyurl.com/6bbfjl.

6. Petty, "Church-to-Church Collaborations."

7. John R. W. Stott, *Christian Mission in the Modern World* (Downers Grove, IL: InterVarsity, 1975), 30.

8. Christopher Quinn, "Sex-Trafficking Fight Goes beyond Streets," *Atlanta Journal-Constitution*, June 15, 2009, https://tinyurl.com/u6ow34b.

9. Chip Sweney, personal interview with Eric Swanson, July 14, 2009.

10. Past Winners: Spirit of Portland Award, https://tinyurl.com/uvn9wna.

11. As told to Eric Swanson by Kevin Palau.

12. Phill Butler, *Well Connected: Releasing Power, Restoring Hope through Kingdom Partnerships* (Waynesboro, GA: Authentic Media, 2005), 34–35.

## Chapter 7
### Systems: They Create Paradigms, Not Programs

1. Jim Collins, "Turning Goals into Results: The Power of Catalytic Mechanisms," *Harvard Business Review*, July–August 1999, https://tinyurl.com/t2pqcr5.
2. Jim Collins, "The Most Creative Product Ever," *Inc.*, May 1997, https://tinyurl.com/wrpcclt.
3. D. Michael Henderson, *A Model for Making Disciples: John Wesley's Class Meeting* (Nappanee, IN: Evangel, 1997), 19.
4. Henderson, *Model for Making Disciples*, 23.
5. Henderson, *Model for Making Disciples*, 28.
6. Charles Edward White and Robby Butler, "John Wesley's Church Planting Movement: Discipleship That Transformed a Nation and Changed the World," *Mission Frontiers* newsletter (US Center for World Missions, September -October 2011).
7. Henderson, *Model for Making Disciples*, 30.
8. Jim Wallis, *God's Politics: Why the Right Gets It Wrong and the Left Doesn't Get It* (San Francisco: HarperSan Francisco, 2006), 212.
9. Mariners Outreach, "History of Local Ministries," marinerschurch.org.
10. Henderson, *Model for Making Disciples*, 48–49.
11. Glen Brechner, Next Big Idea conference, Baylor University, February 10, 2009.
12. Don Simmons, speech, Leadership Community gathering, Dallas, Texas, September 18, 2008.
13. From the transcribed notes of Eric Swanson, May 19, 2009 listening to Matt Carter speak on Missional small groups at a Leadership Network event at which he was a part.
14. Eric Hoffer, *The True Believer: Thoughts on the Nature of Mass Movements* (New York: HarperCollins, 1989), 120. Originally published 1951.

## Chapter 8
### Evangelism: They Deploy Kingdom Laborers, Not Just Community Volunteers

1. Todd Rhoades, email to Eric Swanson, July 30, 2008.
2. Robert D. Lupton, *Theirs Is the Kingdom: Celebrating the Gospel in Urban America* (San Francisco: HarperOne, 2011), 50.
3. John Stott and Christopher J. H. Wright, *Christian Mission in the Modern World*, Updated and expanded ed. (Downers Grove, IL: InterVarsity, 2015), 30.
4. Dave Gibbons, Leadership Network's Camp Improv, Dallas, Texas, October 1, 2003.
5. Ben Ecklu, Global City Movement meeting, Montserrat, Spain, June 29, 2008.

6. See "Fresh Coat Cleveland Channel 23 Newscast," YouTube video, July 17, 2007, https://tinyurl.com/wbawd4o.

7. From a conversation with Ian Vickers in Leadership Network, *Kingdom Impact Report* (internal document).

8. Steve Sjogren, David Ping, and Doug Pollock, *Irresistible Evangelism* (Loveland, CO: Group Publishing, 2004).

9. David Kinnaman and Gabe Lyons, *UnChristian: What a New Generation Really Thinks about Christianity . . . and Why It Matters* (Grand Rapids, MI: Baker, 2007), 25.

10. Steve Sjogren, David Ping, and Doug Pollock, *Irresistible Evangelism* (Loveland, CO: Group Publishing, 2004), 5, with minor modifications.

11. Hal Seed, email to Eric Swanson, September 23, 2004.

12. Brian Mavis and Rick Rusaw, *The Neighboring Church: Getting Better at What Jesus Says Matters Most* (Nashville, TN: Thomas Nelson, 2016).

13. *Reviving Evangelism: Current Realities That Demand a New Vision for Sharing Faith* (The Barna Group, 2019).

14. Don Everts and Dough Schaupp, *I Once Was Lost: What Postmodern Skeptics Taught Us about Their Path to Jesus* (Downers Grove, IL: IVP Academic, 2008).

15. Guy Kawasaki, "The Art of Evangelism," Guy Kawasaki website, January 12, 2006, https://tinyurl.com/yxy272zv.

## Chapter 9
## Creativity: They Innovate, Not Replicate

1. Leadershipnetwork, "Innovative Churches Are Different," YouTube, July 30, 2009, https://tinyurl.com/uolwe23.

2. Tom Kelley and Jonathan Littman, *The Ten Faces of Innovation: Ideos's Strategies for Beating the Devil's Advocate and Driving Creativity throughout Your Organization* (New York: Doubleday, 2005), 6.

3. Quoted in Kermit Pattison, "How to Kill an Idea," *Fast Company*, May 30, 2008, https://tinyurl.com/vuyncch.

4. Elaine Dundon, *The Seeds of Innovation: Cultivating the Synergy That Fosters New Ideas* (New York: AMACOM, 2002), 6.

5. Sonal Chokshi, ed., "Google X Head of Moonshots: 10x is Easier Than 10 Percent," February 11, 2013, https://tinyurl.com/vyyjx37.

6. Quoted in Stephen Shields, *Churches in Missional Renaissance: Facilitating the Transition to a Missional Mind-Set* (unpublished Leadership Network paper), August 12, 2008.

7. Lindsay Melvin, "Isaac Hayes Service Prompts Outcry," *Memphis Commercial Appeal*, August 14, 2008,

8. Eli Morris, email to Eric Swanson, Mar. 26, 2009.

9. First Presbyterian Church Boulder, Colorado, "For Boulder with Love" (Boulder, CO: First Pres Boulder, 2019), 7.
10. Christian Smith, Michael O. Emerson, and Patricia Snell, *Passing the Plate: Why American Christians Don't Give Away More Money* (New York: Oxford University Press, 2008), 52.
11. Smith, Emerson, and Snell, *Passing the Plate*, 52.
12. Matt Vande Bunte, "Study Says Church Giving Lacks External Focus," Religion News Service, January 9, 2007, https://tinyurl.com/urmt756.
13. Emilie Burk, "Is There a Statute of Limitations on Medical Debt?, Money Management International, November 14, 2018, https://tinyurl.com/v9fdm8s.
14. Madeline Mitchell, "Crossroads Church Leverages Donations to Wipe Out $46.5 Million in Medical Debt," *Cincinnati Enquirer*, February 24, 2020, https://tinyurl.com/vkfcacq.
15. Mitchell, "Crossroads Church Leverages Donations."
16. Kenneth Burke, "How Many Texts Do People Send Every Day (2018)?," Text Request, May 18, 2016, https://tinyurl.com/y82dustj.
17. Independent Sector, "Value of Volunteer Time Rose 3 Percent in 2018," *Philanthropy News Digest*, April 23, 2019, https://tinyurl.com/u4rzjdf.
18. Peter Drucker, *Innovation and Entrepreneurship* (New York: Harper Business, 2006), 19.
19. W. Chan Kim and Renée Mauborgne, *Blue Ocean Strategy* (Brighton, MA: Harvard Business Review Press, 2015), 4.
20. This idea stems from a conversation between Eric Swanson and Erwin McManus at Mosaic in July 2003.
21. William James, https://tinyurl.com/sq2wck6.
22. Quoted in Tricia Armstrong, *The Whole-Brain Solution: Thinking Tools to Help Students Observe, Make Connections and Solve Problems* (Portland, ME: Stenhouse, 2003), 80.

## Chapter 10
## Outcomes: It's about the Game, Not the Pregame Talk

1. As confirmed to Eric by Norwood Davis, March 9, 2020.
2. Carol Sparge, "Early Christmas: church pays off $62K in school lunch debt for students in need," WFTV9 ABC, December 12, 2019, https://tinyurl.com/t4sbth8.
3. Fellowship Bible Church, "The Only Life Worth Living: Shoe Sunday," Sermon, September 18, 2005.
4. Dennis Keating, personal communication, August 21, 2009.
5. Lester M. Salamon (Editor), *The State of Nonprofit America* (Washington D.C.: Brookings Institute Publishing, 2002), 409.
6. Thomas Paine, "Introduction," *Common Sense* (1776).

7. Jim Collins, *Good to Great and the Social Sectors* (New York: HarperCollins, 2005), 5, 7.
8. Collins, *Good to Great*, 5, 7.
9. W. David Phillips, "Re-Imagining Success," blog post, June 6, 2008, https://tinyurl.com/wq85tj7.
10. Tyler VanderWeele, "On the Promotion of Human Flourishing," presentation at Sixth IECO – RCC International Colloquium, Harvard, YouTube video, May 8, 2018, https://tinyurl.com/tsz9hts.
11. Tyler J. VanderWeele, "On the Promotion of Human Flourishing," PNAS, August 1, 2017, https://tinyurl.com/vde883h, 8150.
12. VanderWeele, "On the Promotion," 8151.
13. Peter F. Drucker, *Managing the Nonprofit Organization* (New York: HarperCollins, 1998), xiv.